A PERSONAL NOTE FROM DR. ROBERT ANTHONY...

Dear Professional Speaker,

I have, to the best of my ability, covered everything I know about the speaking and seminar business in this book. The opportunities that await you as a professional speaker are tremendous. Admittedly, taking the first step is the most difficult of all. But once you've started, each step will get easier and easier.

This book is a summary of my 12 years' experience as a successful speaker and seminar promoter. I urge you to use my experience resulting from years of trial, error, and set-backs to your advantage.

Keep referring to this book. Once you have the knowledge of the basics, the odds are in your favor. I sincerely hope you will be inspired to use this manual as a constant source of practical information and guidance as you continue to build a lucrative paid speaking and seminar business.

Best wishes,

Robert Anthony

HOW TO MAKE A FORTUNE FROM PUBLIC SPEAKING

PUT YOUR MONEY WHERE YOUR MOUTH IS

DR. ROBERT ANTHONY

B

BERKLEY BOOKS, NEW YORK

This Berkley book contains the complete
text of the original edition.
It has been completely reset in a typeface
designed for easy reading and was printed
from new film.

HOW TO MAKE A FORTUNE FROM PUBLIC SPEAKING:
PUT YOUR MONEY WHERE YOUR MOUTH IS

A Berkley Book / published by arrangement with
Robear Corporation

PRINTING HISTORY
Previously published by New Thought Publications, Inc.
Robear edition published 1983
Berkley edition / August 1985

ISBN: 0-425-11327-2

A BERKLEY BOOK ® TM 757,375
Berkley Books are published by The Berkley Publishing Group,
200 Madison Avenue, New York, New York 10016.
The name "BERKLEY" and the "B" logo
are trademarks belonging to Berkley Publishing Corporation.
PRINTED IN THE UNITED STATES OF AMERICA

10 9 8 7 6 5 4 3

CONTENTS

INTRODUCTION

During the 12 years I have been in the speaking and seminar business, I have seen highly qualified and competent speakers unable to make a living as full time professional speakers. Their programs were well put together, contained worthwhile information, and their presentations were highly suited to a successful career in the speaking and seminar business. On the other hand, I have seen speakers who had mediocre material and a poor presentation make big money as professional speakers. On the surface this seems unfair, until you are aware of the key factor that determines the ultimate success or failure in the speaking and seminar business. Here it is:

Your success in the speaking and seminar business will be determined more by your *ability to market and promote yourself* than by your program content or presentation.

When I first set out to become a professional speaker, I thought that all I had to do was learn how to present a good speech or a good seminar and I would be able to make a living as a professional speaker.

A good program and an effective presentation *are not sufficient for success in this business*. Perhaps it shouldn't be that way but that's the way it is. Most people are not aware of this when they start out. They believe a good message and an effective presentation is their key to success. They soon find out that having a great message and delivery is only *part* of what it takes to make a living as a professional speaker.

In the long run you will need a quality program and an effective presentation, but the bottom line for success in the speaking and seminar business lies in your ability to market and promote yourself. This book is designed to help you market and promote yourself as a professional speaker. It focuses on clearing away the obstacles that will confront you in building a lucrative professional paid speaking business. The potential for success in this business is enormous. The demand for speeches, seminars, and training programs is growing every day. Adult education is the fastest growing business in America today. Make no mistake about it, this is a highly competitive business but there is plenty of room for creative people who have something to say, the ability to communicate it, and know-how to market and to promote their services. This book was written to give you practical, current and tested information on how to do this.

My purpose in writing this book (aside from making

a few extra dollars!) is to assist you in getting started or to improve your ability to market and promote yourself as a professional speaker. To the best of my ability I will show you how to invest your time, energy, and money so that you can reap the highest possible rewards for your efforts.

If you follow the instructions and suggestions based on my experience and the experience of others that I have learned from, you will be able to avoid the pitfalls that most people experience when getting started as a professional speaker. You have taken the first step by purchasing this book. Congratulations! The next step is to read through the pages and follow the instructions and suggestions very carefully. Take your time and do what needs to be done step-by-step. Don't try to take any shortcuts. If you do, it will only delay your success. You will not become a successful speaker overnight. It takes time, commitment, and that unpopular word "work".

The most important piece of advice I have for you at this point is to enjoy the trip. Life is not a destination. Life is a journey. The rewards and satisfaction come more from enjoying the trip along the way than from the actual achievement.

You have, I believe, that human urge for the better things in life which is common to all successful individuals. You desire an outlet for your talents so that you can experience your full potential. The speaking and seminar business will enable you to develop your own inner potential while helping others to develop theirs. In the process you will grow in consciousness, meet interesting people and make a lot of money! In essence, you will experience the best life has to offer. In order to do that, you have to learn the rules and tools. With this in mind it's time to get started on that magnificent journey!

WHO HIRES SPEAKERS

There are two basic ways speakers are hired. The first is to be engaged by a business, group, or organization which generally pays a *set fee* based on the length of the speech, seminar, or workshop presented by the speaker. The second method is to be paid on a *per person basis* which is calculated by the *number of people* present in the audience rather than a set fee determined in advance.

I plan to address many of the specific organizations which you may wish to contact, but here are just a few possibilities:

1. Business and trade organizations
2. Civic groups
3. Convention planners
4. Service organizers
5. Business firms and corporations
6. Political affiliations

7. **Fraternal organizations**
8. **Athletic clubs**
9. **Professional associations**
10. **Church groups**

Of course, the types of organizations you choose will be tailored to your own program content and presentation. You will be pleasantly surprised at the enormous number of organizations you probably never knew existed as you scan the yellow pages of the phone directory or of the various reference sources available in the public library. The problem will not then be to find an organization to engage your services, but to decide which one to choose.

Another method is to promote your own speeches, seminars, and/or workshops to the *general public* in a variety of ways. Instead of, or in addition to contracting a specific organization, you may choose to do this. Later in this book I shall discuss the advantages as well as the drawbacks of promoting your program to the general public.

HOW MUCH MONEY
CAN YOU MAKE AS A SPEAKER?

If you are promoting your own programs to the general public, your income will be determined by how skilled you are in marketing yourself. Once again, I cannot over-emphasize this fact . . . Regardless of the quality of your presentation, it does you absolutely no good whatsoever if you are speaking to an empty room. The fees I mention in this section are totally within the realm of possibility; they are realistic, but only and I repeat *only* with the proper marketing.

The first check I received for speaking professionally was $100.00. It seemed like a million dollars to me at the time. The truth of the matter is I thought I was being overpaid! Today I receive in excess of $3000.00 per day! This is my *minimum* fee for a full day.

I can assure you that your first check, regardless of the amount, will be a thrill. You see, it will be the first reward you receive for so painstakingly having perfected your craft without pay. Your very first payday as a public speaker is most significant; you are now a professional. From that day forward your fees will continue to rise slowly or they will soar depending upon your ability to market yourself.

Read carefully what I have written about my fees and those of other speakers. Formulate an idea of what type of fees you want and are willing to accept for yourself. Remember that you have something worthwhile to say, to contribute, and you most definitely should be well paid for sharing your knowledge with your audience.

The highest paid people are the celebrity speakers. Johnny Carson receives $40,000 and Henry Kissinger receives $35,000 for each speech they give! .Most speakers receive considerably less. However, many of their incomes are far above the average medical doctor or corporate executive. It is not unusual to earn $100,000 to $500,000 per year as a professional speaker.

Make no mistake about it, professional speakers are among the highest paid people in the world. *A Professional* speaker with a minimum of experience can charge the following fees:

$ 500.00 for a one hour speech.

$ 700.00 for an out of area speech where there is travel involved. The extra $200.00 is for your travel *time*. You must charge for your expenses on top of the $700.00.

$ 1000.00 for a local half day program.

$ 1200.00 for an out of area half day program. Plus expenses.

$ 1200.00 for a local full day program. Plus expenses.

It is important never to overlook your *expenses*. I almost tended to do this in the beginning as I was flying to places I had always wanted to visit, eating in fine restaurants, staying in comfortable hotels. I was constantly saying to myself, "I can't believe they are really paying me to do this!" Keep this in mind, *you are entitled to your expenses* and the organizations which hire you are *used to paying them*. If, however, you do not bring this up, chances are they may not. Remember, paying your expenses out of your own pocket when the hiring association is expected to do so, is not only foolish but it's a poor business practice.

There are other factors involved in setting your fees, such as how many people will be there. This is always an important consideration. Sometimes your fee is set on a *per person* basis. If the organization you are working with does not have the budget to pay your fee but still wants you to speak, you will have to work out a *per person cost* based on how many people will be there so that you will receive your standard fee plus expenses.

The above fees are *minimum* fees for beginning speakers who have had some experience but are not well known to the public. More money comes with one thing, and this is something you must dedicate yourself to if you are going to make it big in the speaking and seminar business. *YOU MUST BECOME FA-*

MOUS. The more famous you are, the more money you will be paid for doing the same speech or seminar. If you don't work on becoming famous, you will only be able to command the minimum fee. On top of that, you probably won't have much work because the general public will be unfamiliar with who you are and what you do.

Making yourself famous is something you have to work on *every day* if you want to build a lucrative paid speaking business. Starting now it must be part of your personal goal planning.

If you are a professional speaker with a quality program and an effective presentation, you have two choices:

1. You can remain *low-profile*, sharing your wonderful message with various organizations for a minimal fee . . . or . . .

2. You can work towards *celebrity status* (within various frames of reference) and share *exactly* the same message for big bucks.
SO LET'S GET FAMOUS!!!!!

HOW TO BECOME FAMOUS

The fastest way to build your name and become famous is to get *published*. Perhaps you are conjuring up images of novelists who send manuscripts to dozens of book publishers each week and consider themselves fortunate if they even receive a rejection. Book publishers receive far more manuscripts than you or I can even begin to imagine. Most of these manuscripts never get read, let alone published.

With editors of *magazines*, however, it is an entirely different story. They are constantly looking for new material and are most eager for contributions from talented, fresh sources. Bear in mind that they must have new material to fill their periodical month after month or better yet, week after week.

Be honest with yourself. Haven't you at least at one time or another read a magazine article and thought to yourself, "I could write something which would be of far greater interest to the readers of this periodical"? And in all probability you are correct. And yet what is the basic difference between you and the person who wrote that article? That person took action. Right?

I know many "authors" with manuscripts for the great American novel sitting on their desks at home and yet, every single person I know who has *persistently* submitted articles to magazines has been published. Getting published is a numbers game. To be in the numbers you have to submit articles. So start now by submitting article #1. You will be pleasantly surprised to find that eventually your article will be accepted and published.

You must write articles that your potential clients will read in trade publications. You can get books from the library that list all the associations in the United States. Ask the librarian for the *Encyclopedia of Associations*. What you want to look for are associations which would be interested in the kind of speeches or programs you have to offer. Most of these associations have trade publications.

Another excellent source for trade publications is the *International Directory of Little Magazines and Small Presses* published by Dustbooks.

After you pick the publications you want to work with, contact them by phone. Call . . . don't write. Talk to the editor of the magazine and tell him or her who you are and that you have written an article that would be of interest to his readers. Have the *title* of the article in mind so that you can give it to him if he asks.

You may want to give a brief synopsis of what is included in your article to further arouse interest. The article will not be an end-all in itself but will convince the readers that you are an authority of your subject matter and will stimulate them to learn more about you and your program.

Many of these magazines will also pay you a fee so they are actually *paying you* for the privilege of advertising your business. Writing articles for magazines not only helps you to become famous but it provides an extra source of income.

You can write one article and change the title and some of the content so that it can be submitted to several publications. Remember, the more articles you submit, the greater the chances will be of having your article published.

When submitting your articles to the various publications, *Never* under any circumstances do so without including your picture. So many speakers make this mistake and are missing out on yet another perfect opportunity to become well-known. People respond very well to visuals and you want them to be able to correlate what you have written with your appearance. Studies have proven that they will be more likely to remember you if they have seen your picture with the article. In fact, it is an excellent idea to put your picture on everything that has your name on it such as your business cards and stationery. The name of the game is, "Don't forget me."

After you have made contact with the editor of a magazine and he agrees to read your article, send it to him in the mail. *Send it to the publication in care of him*. In a week or so call him back. If he doesn't use your article or hasn't read it right away, keep calling him until you get *results*. You don't want to be pushy but you do want to be persistent. If you will do this, you will get your articles published in several publications.

When you do get your articles published, make copies of them because you will need them for your press kit. This will help you to become more famous.

The speakers who become well-known are the speakers who are *different*. Your program can be very similar in content to that of other speakers, however, you must find a way to distinguish *yourself* from the thousands of other individuals who call themselves professional speakers. There is nothing worse in this business than to hear someone in charge of hiring a speaker say, "There is no sense in having Mr. White, he's just like Mr. Grey and we heard him two months ago." Don't be like Grey . . . or anybody else for that matter. *Be different!* Find a way to develop your own style.

Give serious thought to just what you will do with your material and/or presentation that others have not done. Observe other speakers, attend their presentations and study exactly what it is in the material and delivery that causes you to remember some and not others. Learn to be different, novel, innovative. Think about some of the outrageous TV and showbusiness personalities. Maybe *you* wouldn't pay to see them but they *are* getting bookings. Be controversial if you have to be, but find a way to stand out from the crowd.

Never ignore any possible situation where you might get your name known. Talk to people in public places, pass out your business cards, and constantly promote yourself. Notice I said *Yourself*. It is imperative that you promote *yourself* rather than your program. We are certainly not ignoring the value of what you have to say but it will never get said if you cannot get in front of an audience. You will be able to deliver your message only by first promoting yourself as a "personality". The public wants an *image*. They must become interested in *you* before they become interested in your program.

Why do you think the multi-million dollar corporations use big-name celebrities to endorse everything from automobiles to yogurt? *Identification*. The public must be able to identify with you as a person. Become famous, achieve celebrity status, and the public will pay big money to hear what you couldn't give away free before.

Starting from absolute obscurity, as I well know, can be more than a little discouraging. To use another cliche, but one that is true, "The first step is the hardest." The more you do to become well-known, the more others will do *for* you. Promoting yourself is one thing but having others do it for you simply because they have benefited from your program is the best possible advertising you can get.

I now find myself able to get bookings I wouldn't have had a chance at getting 10 years ago. All because my name is very well-known in my chosen field and one organization constantly recommends me to another. As each day goes by on your journey to fame and fortune, you will find that you will have to reach out less and less and that people will be coming to you more and more. But don't forget, at first *you* must do all the reaching.

Whenever you are going to give a speech or seminar, publicize it as much as possible. If you are different, interesting and informative, the radio, TV and newspapers will be more than willing, in fact eager, to interview you.

Think about the talk shows in your own area for starters. Watch them to see what kinds of guests they have and what subjects are covered. Could you do that? Could you do *better*? Once again, if you are different, they will jump at the chance to invite you to be a guest on their show. If you do a spot on a talk show, promote yourself and your program. Again, the result is free advertising that you could never afford to buy.

Every city to which you travel has similar local shows which should never be ignored as another opportunity to promote yourself. Nor are the national shows such as Hour Magazine entirely out of the realm of possibility. I know several speakers who have been on Hour Magazine and indicated that it was no more difficult to book than their own local talk shows.

If you have a particularly controversial subject, The Donahue Show is a good place for you to book an appearance. It's not as easy to get on the Donahue Show as it is a local show, but don't rule it out. The success of that show depends upon controversial material and interesting personalities. You may be one of them!

Remember to follow these essential points in order to achieve celebrity status as a professional speaker.

1. Have your articles published.
2. Always consent to interviews.
3. Appear on as many talk shows as possible.
4. Include your photo whenever you can.
5. Promote yourself everywhere you go.
6. BE DIFFERENT.

If you follow these 6 suggestions on a day-to-day basis, you will soon be on your way to fame, and shortly thereafter to fortune as well.

LEARNING TO SPEAK

An organization totally dedicated to personal growth and communication excellence is *Toastmasters International*. Comprising the over 4000 clubs in the United States and foreign countries, Toastmasters are community-based, company-based and military clubs.

The club was formed in 1924 "to afford practice and training in the art of public speaking and in presiding over meetings, and to promote sociability and good fellowship among its members."

Most Toastmaster clubs meet weekly and there are breakfast, lunch, dinner, and evening meetings to accommodate a variety of job situations. Regardless of where you live, it is probable that you will find at least one Toastmaster club in your community.

Members of the club receive not only numerous occasions to present formal speeches but to speak extemporaneously, to serve as Toastmaster, to provide humor and to fulfill various other functions at the weekly meetings. The learning experience results from the feedback of the other Toastmasters, as well as listening to their presentations.

A variety of materials are available to members of the club, many of which could be helpful to you in building your paid speaking and seminar business. Manuals with such titles as "How to use Gestures," "Specialty Speeches," "The Entertaining Speaker," and "Hold Your Audience" are available from headquarters. The monthly magazine features valuable articles, all related to some aspect of public speaking. In addition, self-study cassette programs as well as other ideas and information are available to speakers on all levels.

Toastmasters is a suitable organization for the novice speaker, the veteran, or anyone in between. It is an excellent way to perfect your craft in a positive and relaxed atmosphere. Being a professional paid speaker is not a prerequisite for joining. In fact many members never do speak professionally. They simply wish to use better communication in their personal lives or business careers.

Others use the club as a stepping stone to their public speaking careers. Still others remain in the club long after they begin paid speaking careers. It enables them to keep in touch with other speakers on a continuing basis and to constantly sharpen their skills. One of the most well-known and sought-after national speakers, Cavett Roberts, is still active in Toastmasters.

I only wish that someone had told me about this organization when I was getting started in my speaking career. I am certain that they could have helped me to develop much more quickly the skills that have taken years of trial and error to acquire.

Toastmasters International has and continues to make valuable contributions to public speaking training. If you are interested in learning more about this organization, you may contact the local chapter or write to them at their world headquarters:

> Toastmasters International
> 2200 North Grand Avenue
> Santa Ana, Ca. 92711

NATIONAL SPEAKERS ASSOCIATION

The National Speakers Association is made up of thousands of professional and aspiring speakers throughout the country. It's divided into chapters with a local chapter in almost every major city in the U.S. Most chapters meet on a monthly basis. You can learn the name of the president of your local chapter by writing to their headquarters in Phoenix.

The National Speakers Association does not book speakers but provides training and resource materials for the professional speaker. By joining the National Speakers Association you will have an opportunity to meet other famous and less famous speakers, hear them speak, and share ideas with them.

There is a certain prestige being associated with a national organization. You can use the logo and affiliation with the National Speakers Association on your letterhead, business cards, and promotional material. This will help add to your credibility as a professional speaker.

Through the National Speakers Association you will meet people who are doing what you are doing, share information, and learn from one another. You will find that most professional speakers are more than willing to share their knowledge and experience with their contemporaries. By helping another speaker, a professional understands that he is also helping himself in the process.

You want to train yourself to learn everything you can from people that are already doing what you want to be doing. Associating yourself with this organization will keep you updated on any changes and trends in the world of public speaking. If you want to fly like an eagle, you have to hang around with eagles! You can contact the National Speakers Association by writing to:

> National Speakers Association
> 5201 N. 7th Street
> Phoenix, Az 85014

MAKING UP YOUR "PRESS KIT"

If you wish to successfully prospect your potential clients you will have to put together a "press kit." A press kit is similar to a model's portfolio in that it enables the prospective client to know you well enough to want to engage your services without ever having met you personally. Your press kit is an attractive folder that contains information on *who you are* and *what you do*. It should be sent in advance to the organizations where you would like to secure speaking engagements.

Your press kit will be your prospect's first introduction to you, so every item in it should sell *you*. It should create the image you want your prospect to have of you. When making up your press kit keep this word foremost in your mind: QUALITY. You must look *successful*. No one wants to hire a person who is struggling to get to the top. *It must look like you're already there!* The feeling you want to create is that you are an experienced, accomplished, competent, and successful speaker.

You may be nervously anticipating your first payday as a public speaker or you may have some limited experience. In either case, the recipient of your press kit must believe that you are already a successful speaker. Everything in your kit should reinforce this idea. Once your press kit works for you the first time, you will see that it works even better for you the next time and each time thereafter. With each speaking engagement you can change your press kit, building and adding more information about your experience, expertise, and proficiency as a speaker.

Your press kit should include the following items:

1. *Letters of recommendation*—These are letters from companies, groups, and associations that have worked with you. In the beginning you will only have a few sources to draw from because you will have had a limited amount of speaking engagements. But as time goes on you will have an excellent source on which to draw your best letters. Keep changing the letters and updating your press kit with the most current and most effective letters of recommendation.

Your problem at this point may be that you have no letters at all. The solution is quite simple. Get out and deliver some dynamic interesting talks to as many civic or social organizations as you possibly can. You are doing them a favor by sharing your insight and knowledge with them; the only thing you ask in return is a letter of recommendation. You will be pleased to learn that they will recommend you without hesitation. And there you have it, item #1 in your press kit!

When you ask organizations to write letters of recommendation for you, they will frequently ask, "What do you want me to say?" Plan this carefully in advance and tell them exactly what to say. In some cases you can even outline or write the letter *for* them and they will put it on their own stationery. This may sound contrived, but believe me, those writing the letters will be extremely grateful if you will give them some guidelines to follow.

2. *A biography*—Have a written biography of your education, business background, and your accomplishments. Compiling this may seem like quite a chore, but remember how you managed when applying for your very first job? It may have been years ago and you are a bit out of practice, but that certainly can be overcome by the fact that you have had many experiences and achievements since that time which you can now include.

Remember that you cannot possibly be physically in front of every prospective client so your biography must tell them, "I am interesting, talented, and worth hiring." A short sketchy biography won't do but then neither will one that reads like an encyclopedia. It must make you look good without becoming tiresome. As you begin compiling this and redoing it, you will instinctively know when you have achieved that goal. Do not overlook anything that will help you to look experienced, accomplished, competent and successful.

3. *A copy of your book* (if you have one)—The best way to get a speaking engagement is to send a copy of your book. If you want to get on a radio or TV talk show for further publicity, the first thing they will ask themselves is whether or not you have written a book. The media shows are introducing you to millions of people and these viewers or listeners will want to know where they can learn more about whatever it is you do. They may immediately rule out your seminar for a variety of reasons: They don't think they can afford it, are not willing to make time for it, or don't consider that you will ever be speaking where they could come to hear you in person. Having their interest aroused by the interview they may, however, make a mental note to purchase your book. This could eventually lead them to your seminar. Even if they never hear you in person, you have sold one more book!

If the book is not in your press kit from the beginning, it should be in your mind. As you progress in your speaking career, the necessity for this will soon become apparent and it will increase your motivation for writing your book. In subsequent sections, I include a step-by-step explanation of how to publish and market your own book.

4. *A sample brochure*—Include your best quality brochure. This obviously will help sell you to those in charge of hiring and ultimately to the participants at the seminar who will recommend you to their friends.

This all leads to future speaking engagements. If used properly, your brochure can be one of your most effective prospecting tools.

I have included a section in this book that explains the do's and don'ts of an effective brochure such as design, graphics, paper quality, typesetting, etc. Read it carefully.

PREPARING YOUR "DEMO TAPE"

A Demo Tape is simply a short cassette recording that can be given to prospective clients so that they can hear a portion of your live presentation. It is not enough to send a press kit that just contains printed material. Most people will hesitate to hire you until they have heard you first. After all, you are in the "speaking" not the "writing" business; the clients *must hear your voice* if you want to win them over. In reality, this should be called an *audition* tape. That's exactly what it is. Just as in auditioning for a play, how well you do determines whether or not you "get the part."

A demo tape should be no longer than 15 minutes in length. This is a sufficient amount of time for someone to get the general feeling of what you sound like and what kind of material you are presenting. My demo tape is only 12 minutes in length because I feel most of my clients are busy people and their time is at a premium. If they know what they want, they will be able to make a decision based on what they have heard during the 12 minute mini-presentation.

To make a demo tape you will need to record several of your live presentations. Listen to the recordings and pick out the parts that represent your best presentation. Try to have as much audience reaction as you possibly can. If you tell a joke, include the audience laughter. If you say something that evokes applause, include that in your tape. You want to show your prospective client that you can inspire, educate, and motivate your audience. You want him to feel that you could have the same effect if you work with his organization.

I urge you to be particularly aware of the entertainment factor. Everyone loves to laugh. It makes your message much more palatable if they can do so even in the educational atmosphere of your program. As participants enter my seminars they frequently do more than allude to the fact that they hope I'll be amusing as well as informative. If the clients know that laughter is an integral part of your program, they will be more likely to hire you.

Your demo tape will be more effective if you have someone introduce you on the tape. The announcer should give a brief introduction and then say something like "Now let's hear (your name) as he talks about (whatever your subject is at that point)." The tape should be a live presentation of your subject matter that was in the lead-in that the announcer gave. The recording of your material could last about 8–10 minutes and then the announcer would break in again. He would comment on the last thing you talked about and tell the listener he can hear more if he contacts you at your phone number and/or address.

If you can find a well-known celebrity to do your introduction, it will have even more impact. The announcer message should last no more than *one minute* at the *beginning* of the tape and *one minute* at the *end*.

You will need a recording studio to work with you on this so that your original tapes can be cut and edited. Most studios have professional announcers that can do your introduction and closing for you. Keep in mind that this may be the most important piece of material your client will receive. All your other materials tell a message *about* you. Your demo tape is you *in person*. Don't skimp here. Make sure your demo tape is first class.

After the initial production, your demo tapes become very cost effective. The final cost will be approximately 75 cents apiece and as an addition to your press kit, will be worth far more. Have at least 25 tapes as an initial supply. Then your supplier should be able to make additional copies for you with a two or three day turn-around time. Booking agents will also need a demo tape if they are going to book you. First the demo tape must sell the booking agent and then he will use it to sell you to his clients.

A demo tape as part of your self-promotion is well worth the effort. Compare this to the large amount of time and money involved if you were to fly to every city where you want to work and audition in person. The tape is always sent in advance as part of the press kit. All the material in your press kit is important, however, your demo tape will be a primary deciding factor in whether your potential client is likely to hire you or not. Follow the suggestions in this section and put together the best possible tape you can produce. Remember, your demo tape is your best salesman.

SETTING YOUR FEE

When you receive a call from a prospective client *do not say you are immediately available*. Never, never say "yes" to a booking. To do this there are some very important questions you must ask your potential client. If he calls and says that he is interested in having you speak at their next meeting or convention on such and such a date you must follow through with:

1. "Wonderful, *How many people will be attending your convention?*" Find out if you are going to be working with a large, medium, or small audience. The size of the audience has much to do with what you will earn for each engagement. Not only how much, but in what manner or from what sources.

2. *"What is the purpose of this convention?"* He might say that it is to motivate his people to sell twice as much as they did last year. You say, "I am happy you called because that's my specialty!" Remember

this . . . whatever they want, that's your *specialty*! You can usually adjust your presentation to fit the client's needs. If you have sent your press kit off to that particular organization, most likely your material would correlate in some way or another with their needs. With a little creativity, it will tie in perfectly.

3. *"How long a speech or program did you have in mind?"* You want to learn whether it is a one hour speech, a half day seminar, or a full day program.

4. *"Are you interested in publicizing this event?"* If he says "yes" say "I can come in a day early and do some publicity for your organization if you can set up some radio, TV, or newspaper interviews. I will do everything I can to promote your organization during the interviews. With this in mind the potential client will then be eager to arrange interviews for you in order to publicize his organization. The result is that you receive much more exposure as advertising for your program than you otherwise would have had. You will be doing double duty that day, promoting yourself and the organization who set up all this media exposure for you. You will usually be able to mention the name of the organization and the event 5 or 6 times during an interview. Don't miss this chance to promote.

5. *"As long as I am coming in earlier would you like me to do a special program for your key people?"* If he says "yes" you can arrange an *additional* fee for this. Sometimes you can add another half day or hour's income to your scheduled speaking fee for an extra program.

6. *"In what way would you like to use my educational materials?* I have some excellent supportive material through my books and tape cassettes. Would you like to include them in a package so that each person receives one or would you prefer to have a table in the back of the room so that we can make them available to those who wish to invest their own money? Either way is fine with me. Which way works best for you?"

This is the best way to make a directive approach to selling your products. You are telling the client that you are definitely going to sell your products one way or the other. And yet you are making it more comfortable for the client in allowing him the final decision as to exactly *how* it is to be handled.

There is no asking or begging. It avoids the awkward question "Can I sell my books and tapes?" You just accept in your mind that they will be sold wherever you speak. If you accept it, they will too!

7. This is an extremely important question . . . *"Who did you have last year?"* You will soon become familiar with the names of your colleagues so you have a better idea of the quality of speaker they are used to hiring. Then you say *"How much did you pay him?"* This gives you an idea of how much they are used to paying for a speaker.

8. *"What is your budget for this year?"* When this is revealed you may learn that they have a budget for more than you were willing to charge them. You certainly want to take advantage of all available income . . . you are worth it!

On the other hand they may have a budget that is less than your normal fee. If they do not have enough money to pay your normal fee there are two things you can do. First, it can help them by finding a way they can make money with you in order to afford your fees. Think of ways you can help them pay your fee by raising money as a result of your being there.

The second is you may wish to lower your fee. This can be especially beneficial to you if it is a large nationwide organization. If you book a convention of real estate agents and speak to the whole convention, you could book individual agencies to present your program. It would be beneficial to speak at a reduced fee if you could follow up with the individual groups within the association.

If they say they have a budget of $1500 then things are simplified for you. You will know what you can charge. If they indicate that they have a budget of $3000 for two speakers you can ask them if they have contracted for the other speaker. If they have not, you could say "I could do two programs for you and this way we can have continuity and put together the most effective training session. How do you feel about this?" The whole idea is to get as much work as you can while you are there. Your program becomes more cost effective and your profit margin increases considerably if you are able to do multi-programs on one travel budget. Do this whenever possible.

The point here is to never say "yes" until you have asked all of these questions. If you say yes right away, you will cheat yourself out of thousands of dollars of additional business. By asking these questions, you not only help yourself but you are assisting your client in putting together the most effective presentation possible.

It helps to understand that a large majority of convention planners are amateurs. They really have no idea how to put together a successful program. They probably were assigned the task of booking speakers and putting together a meeting with little or no instruction on *how to do it*. In spite of good intentions, their idea of a successful seminar may not necessarily coincide with your own. For example, you could possibly find yourself speaking to a relatively large audience who is very pleased with your program and yet make little money, no money, or worse yet, lose money. This is all due to the fact that the fee was not properly set by asking these very important questions.

Since these planners may not have very much experience and lack creative ideas, you can be of further assistance to them by offering your input. Help them to make their program more interesting. Help them to make their decisions. If you are willing to go out of *your* way to help *them*, they will be willing to go out of *their* way to *book* you.

Keep in mind that the convention planners do not work *for* you. So you must work *with* them to be certain that your interests are satisfied in the course of doing the best possible job for them.

USING OTHER PEOPLE TO MARKET YOU

Most speakers book their own speeches and seminars. Others book some of their speeches and seminars and use booking agencies for the remaining percentage.

Booking agencies, or speakers bureaus as they are also called, work with numerous speakers. They receive calls from meeting planners, associations, corporations and businesses that are looking for a specific type of speaker. The booking agent then matches the speaker with the type of presentation requested by the organization.

As a fee for securing the contract, the booking agents receive a percentage of the fee from the speaker; the fee is usually 25–35% of the speaking fee. The organization booking the speaker does not pay for this service. Some booking agents may want a percentage of your tape and book sales as well, but this is negotiable.

The fees charged by these agents are well worth it for three main reasons:

1. They are in constant contact with numerous organizations on a daily basis.

2. The time they spend in securing your booking, leaves you free to do what you do best . . . which of course, is to speak. You only make money when you are speaking.

3. In reality the percentage you pay is less than it appears because the booking agent pays for the costs involved in securing the booking such as secretarial services, postage, and phone calls. In addition to the above, his or her fee is tax deductible.

Although I would advise you not to rely on booking agents exclusively, they can be an excellent source of additional bookings. There are over 200 booking agencies in the U.S. To locate them you will have to go to the yellow pages and look under *booking agencies*, *lecture bureaus*, or *speakers bureaus*. The majority of libraries have yellow pages from all the major cities in the U.S. Copy down the name of the agencies you wish to contact and write to them, including of course your press kit and a demo tape.

Follow this up with a phone call. Don't wait for them to call *you*. If possible make arrangements to meet with them personally. Take them to lunch if you can. A personal contact with a booking agent is usually worth more than the same time and money spent to meet with the convention planner of *one* organization. The reason for this is obvious; the agent can represent you to *many* organizations rather than just *one* organization.

Sell yourself to the booker so he or she can get to know you personally. You want them to be familiar with you. After you do this keep in touch with them so you will be on their mind. If you are true to your goal of being different and unique, you will stand apart from the speakers who merely contact the agents by mail and never follow through. Remember that persistence, not force is the key here.

Before signing up with an agency, ask them what other speakers they represent. This is an excellent way to evaluate the agency. The registration fees for most booking agencies range from $25.00 to several hundred dollars, so you want to decide if it is worth it to you to pay the fee before signing a contract. This is obviously another reason for wanting to meet with the agent in person. It will assist you in making your decision as to whether or not you want them to represent you.

Keep in mind that booking agents make their money on a percentage basis. *If you cannot command at least $500.00 for your presentation, they will not be interested in working with you.* The reason for this is simple. They receive at least 25% of your fee. If you only get $100.00 it is not worth their time and effort. Booking agents are looking for speakers who consistently receive high fees for their speaking assignments. They are more motivated to work for these speakers.

When booking agents secure a contract with their client, they require the client to send a 25–35% down payment. This is the booking agent's fee. As you can see, the booking agents are paid up front. Most of the time you will not have to pay them directly because they collect their fee in advance. Their contract states that the speaker is to be paid the balance on the date of his presentation. The check is made payable to the speaker. Payment includes the balance of the speaking fee plus expenses.

Use as many booking agents as possible. Most booking agents will not use you exclusively. Some speakers have their own agent that works exclusively for them or for one or two other speakers. However, booking agents want to represent as many speakers as possible. The more booking agents you work with the more work you will have.

Booking agents are not going to do all the work *for* you. You will have to do 80% of your own bookings if you want to make a good living in the speaking and seminar business. They can make some initial bookings for you but you should follow through with referrals within the same organization where you are working. Prospect your clients for different departments, groups, cities, etc., within the same organization. All a booking agent can do is open some doors for you. It's up to you to carry the ball from there.

In addition to using the services of booking agencies you may also wish to consider hiring your own booking agent who works exclusively for you on a permanent basis. This person would be part of your staff. Unlike booking agencies, they receive an hourly wage, plus a bonus for securing your bookings and they work exclusively for you.

Some of the most successful speakers I know have their own staff to do a large part of their booking for them. They are paid on a percentage basis as well as an hourly wage; their only job is to spend time on the phone following leads and securing bookings. The press kits, a copy of the book, and a demo tape are sent out in advance from the office. The staff then follows through to secure the speaking engagements. If you have the right person or persons working for you, you can spend most of your time speaking instead of booking. This should be your ultimate goal.

The following publications can be especially helpful to you and your staff in setting up potential booking dates. *World Convention Dates* contains lists of thousands of conventions booked up to 5 years in advance. Included are what person to contact, what city the convention will be held in and what date. You can send for their subscription by writing to: *WORLD CONVENTION DATES 79 Washington Street, Hempstead, N.Y. 11550*

One of the most knowledgeable, competent and creative booking agents in the U.S. today is Dottie Walters. She provides materials and services for the professional speaker and her newsletter is the best in the business. She knows the speaking business from both sides because she is also one of the most sought after and highest paid speakers in America today. I strongly suggest you contact her and ask her to send you a list of her materials and services. She has helped many people with her professional skills and is always receptive to working with the professional speaker. You can contact her by writing to: *Dottie Walters, 18825 Hicrest Rd., Glendora, Ca. 91740*

As you can see, the name of the game in the speaking business is BOOKINGS! You can never have too many bookings but you certainly can have too few. The advantages of each system are apparent, but do not put all your eggs in one basket. If you diligently book yourself, contact agents, and eventually hire your own staff, you will acquire far more bookings than you would depending upon only one source.

REFERRALS

A job well done for one division of a company provides you with the perfect opportunity to get referrals
to *other* divisions. After giving a talk that has been
particularly well received by the organization you
should ask the person who was in charge of hiring
you the following:

> "Would you be willing to allow me to write a letter
> which we would send out on your stationery to some
> of the other managers in this company to tell them
> what we have accomplished here today?"

You must *ask* for this letter. Even though most of the
time those in charge will be more than happy to write
it, you must take the initiative to ask for it. Perhaps
you would hesitate to do this thinking, "They paid my
fee so they don't owe me anything." I can understand
your reluctance, but look at it this way. They would

have had to pay your fee regardless of the *quality* of your presentation. If you give them a quality presentation they will not only be happy to pay your fee but will want to do something *extra* for you. It is a reward for a job well done, comparable to the extra tip received by the waiter or waitress in return for exceptional service.

If you give a good presentation you will generally find them willing to write the letter for two reasons:

1. They look good in their organization for having hired such an excellent speaker.

2. They want the others in their company to benefit from your program just as their division has.

I find that most organizations want to do something extra if they are extremely satisfied. Do not miss this opportunity to get referrals.

When they agree, draft the letter, ask them for some of their letterhead, and send it out on their stationery over the individual's signature. A letter from someone *within the company* is the *most powerful recommendation you can have*. It is stronger than any communication you could possibly initiate yourself.

Because I have never hesitated to ask, I have hundreds of letters in my file that have brought me numerous speaking contracts. You will too!

NEWSLETTERS

A newsletter is one of the finest marketing tools a speaker can use. It's an excellent way of picking up referral business. People who have worked with you or have attended your presentations may forget you in a short time. Worse than having forgotten you, they may not be sure you are still in business. They will have more confidence in referring you to others if they are kept informed of your activity through a newsletter. Your newsletter will remind them of how others are still using your services.

Some possible items to include in your newsletter are:

1. A schedule of where you are speaking.
2. Reviews of book and cassette packages.
3. Articles and information closely related to your program.

A newsletter is also an excellent way to market your

products through mail order. You can build a substantial aftermarket for your books and tapes by including a list and an order form with each newsletter. I am constantly amazed at the orders I receive from individuals who have taken my programs months or years ago because I have kept in touch with them through my newsletter.

It is not necessary to publish a newsletter every month. A high quality newsletter 3 or 4 times a year will produce good results. Remember, anything you print with your name on it should be of the highest quality. Your newsletter is no exception. Many people will see your newsletter that have never heard of you because it was passed on by a friend. This is their first introduction to you, so *look good*!

Newsletters can be time consuming to produce. As with everything else there is a right way and a wrong way to do it. The library has excellent publications in their reference department on how to write and publish a newsletter. If you need additional help, I would suggest contacting Howard Shensen. He has materials that will show how to build your own consulting practice and how to conduct profitable seminars. His material is based on his experience in the seminar and consulting business. You can contact him by writing to: *Howard Shensen, 20121 Ventura Blvd., Woodland Hills, Calif.*

In the event that you do choose to publish a newsletter, you may approach it in one of two ways. The first way is to pass out address cards at your program and those wishing to receive the newsletter will send them in to you. They and anyone else requesting your newsletter would receive it free of charge. On the other hand you may wish to build this into a subscription service and charge a set annual fee. Either way it will be extremely helpful in building your product aftermarket and more importantly will introduce your products and services to individuals, businesses or groups who may never have heard of you before. A newsletter is a wise investment for the professional speaker.

PUTTING TOGETHER YOUR PROGRAM

Public or In-house?

There are two ways to present your program. The first way is to have your participants come to you. This would be a seminar or workshop that is open to the public. Your advertising, marketing and promotion would be targeted to a certain segment of the general public that would have a potential interest in your subject matter. Your compensation would be based on how many people you could interest in signing up for your program.

The second way to present your program is for you to go to your audience. This would be an in-house seminar. The organization you are working with would set up and provide an audience for you based on an agreed compensation arrangement. You would know in advance what to expect as far as your compensation is concerned.

The in-house seminar provides a greater element of financial security. However, the public seminar can provide a much larger income if promoted properly. Both have their advantages. We will discuss the successful application of both methods in this section.

Successful speeches, seminars and workshops are currently being given on every subject imaginable. There are self improvement seminars, investing seminars, psychic seminars, nutrition seminars and even seminars on how to give seminars! The list is endless. Some of these are low budget lectures given in inexpensive rented rooms. Some of them are given in lavish hotels and retreat centers; the others fall somewhere in between.

The length of the programs can range from a one hour speech to a week long training program. There is no such thing as a standard presentation.

I have seen programs so rigidly structured that you couldn't go to the bathroom without permission to those so casually put together you would have difficulty distinguishing the leader from the participants.

How can you determine if your program has a chance for success in this myriad of presentations? First of all, there is no way that you can determine *in advance* if your program will be a success or a failure in the marketplace. You can spend untold hours speculating, contemplating and calculating the potential success of your program but there is no way to know for sure until you *test market your program*.

Testing Before Investing

If there is one motto a speaker should tack over his desk, it's this: *I WILL TEST BEFORE I INVEST*. Before you invest your hard earned money in full scale promotion you must test to see if your program has the necessary profit potential to be successful. That is, you must actually promote, market and conduct your program on a limited budget before an audience to evaluate results of your marketing techniques and the receptivity to your material. You do not have to risk your life savings to do this. In fact, you can keep your initial testing to a modest, manageable level if you know what to do and how to do it.

Test marketing can help you to determine what the public demand will be for your program and what changes you will need to make to effectively market it. Using low overhead and start up costs in a *local* test market will enable you to get an idea of the potential your program has on a *national* basis. You can do this inexpensively. A test run on a local basis can be accomplished on a budget of $500–$600.

Approximately two thirds of your expenses in presenting your seminar will be spent on your "acquisition costs." Your acquisition cost is the amount of money you must spend to attract each participant. An example would be if you budgeted $500.00 to promote your seminar and 100 people signed up for your program. Your acquisition cost per person would be $5.00. The acquisition cost per person is the largest single factor in determining the profit potential for your program.

If you advertise in the newspaper you must learn from testing how many qualified prospects your ad will draw and what the acquisition cost per person will be. Before placing your ad you must determine if the people you wish to attract read the publication where you are advertising. If you use direct mail you must target your likely prospects before sending out expensive mailings.

It is important to be constantly aware of the pulling power of your advertising and promotion. Some publications which in the beginning seem like a "sure thing" many times will not pull enough registrants to justify their cost. On the other hand, if you test market your advertising carefully you will discover advertising sources that you may not have thought were likely sources.

Major publishers and mail order companies know the value of testing before investing. Every time I mail order a new item I test it very carefully on a small scale to see if it has long term profit potential. There are several large book companies that advertise a book before it is written to test if the book has profit potential. If they receive a poor response they contact the customers and provide them with a reason for canceling their order and include a refund.

It would be nice if you could do this in the speaking and seminar business but there is no way you can successfully get away with it. You can't advertise your program and if enough people don't show up just tell the ones who did show up that you were "just testing to see how many people would show up." You can imagine their reaction. You would be lucky to get away with just a harsh verbal thrashing.

Your initial program should be inexpensive and simply designed so that you can make changes quickly and inexpensively by responding to the feedback you receive from your marketing, promotion and actual presentation. Your audience is the best source of feedback you can have.

When I first started giving seminars I thought all I had to do was to put together a decent program and advertise it to the general public. I believed that most people would be interested in attending my program. So I placed my ads and no one showed up! I soon learned what needed to be changed and what needed to be expanded. The point is that there is no way to know in advance until you test market your idea first.

Testing will allow you to conserve your capital for a major expansion once your program content, advertising and marketing techniques have been refined. In the beginning you will be able to make changes inexpensively. It is not necessary to spend thousands of dollars to market your program. You can get started with a modest investment if you are willing to start slowly and take the necessary steps to refine your presentation and marketing techniques. In effect you

are starting your program "off Broadway." Once you
have refined your promotion, marketing and presentation you're ready for the big time.

Your flexibility and willingness to test and make
changes will put you far ahead of the competition who
thinks all you have to do is to make up a fancy brochure, place big ads, and wait for the people to flock
to your seminar. The largest single mistake that people
make in the speaking and seminar business, that will
put them out of business immediately is *they think
everyone is a potential prospect for their presentation*.
If this were true everyone who entered the speaking
and seminar business would be a success.

The two most difficult obstacles that you will have to
overcome in the speaking and seminar business are:

  1. Targeting your audience.
  2. Promoting and marketing your services.

These are not insurmountable obstacles. They can be
overcome if you carefully follow the suggestions and
instructions in this manual. At this point I just want
you to be aware of them so your mind can center and
focus on the solution instead of the problem.

WHAT TO CALL YOUR PROGRAM

Your ability to market and promote yourself will be strongly influenced by what you decide to call your program. A successful program title should consist of the following two elements:

Who you are

If possible your name should be part of the title of your program. The purpose of this is not ego, but *association*. You want your participants to associate *you* with your *subject matter*. It is much easier to sell a program when it is attached to a personality than one that just states the subject matter. Tying your name to the program helps the participants to realize there is a real person behind the program. The best way to achieve this is to attach *your name* to the title of your program.

What you do

Your title should correspond as closely as possible to
your subject matter. If you are presenting a success
training seminar, you should state that in your title.
Don't call it something else just to be clever.

An example of combining the above two elements
would be the "JOHN DOE SUCCESS TRAINING
PROGRAM." It's not catchy but it will draw more
participants than calling your program "SUCCESS IN
THE 80'S" OR "NEW AGE SUCCESS PROGRAM."

I have noticed that Dale Carnegie now uses both elements. They have the Dale Carnegie Sales Training
Program, Dale Carnegie Management Program, etc.
The Dale Carnegie success story is a legend. Learn
from their experience. When deciding what to call
your program, remember to include *who you are* and
what you do in the title. It will help your participants
to identify you with your program. This in turn helps
you to become more famous and as we said earlier,
more "Fame" means more $$$.

CHOOSING YOUR TOPIC

The broader the appeal of your topic the easier it will be to promote. Try to put together your presentation in such a way the highest number of people would be interested. Not only would they be interested in your subject matter but they would be willing to pay you for more information.

You can increase your chances for success if you choose a subject that *personally interests you*. One that you are highly versed in and one you will want to continually study and develop. The best subject would be one that you could talk on for several hours on a minute's notice. It should be one that thoroughly excites you. If your topic is intrinsically interesting to you it will be easier to deliver with enthusiasm and conviction to your audience. Believe me, you can't fool your audience. They will know right away by your voice, delivery and body language how interested you are in your subject matter. Over 60% of our communication is non-verbal. The more committed you are to your topic the greater your chance of success will be as a professional speaker.

Ther are some additional considerations that must be addressed in choosing your topic. They are:

1. *Is there a long-term demand for your topic?* Will people still be interested in your subject matter 5–7 years from now? You will have a much better chance for success if you choose a topic that will have a long term sustained interest. Stay away from subjects that are fads or have limited appeal.

2. *Are people willing to pay for the information you have to offer on this topic?* If you can show a person that they can make more money or become more successful in their occupation they will consider your presentation a cost effective investment worth paying for. For the most part they would be willing to pay you for this information out of their own pocket. Keep this in mind: no one wants to pay for information or training that they perceive will benefit others more than themselves. If they feel their employer will benefit more from your program they will not be receptive to paying for it out of their own pocket. In this case you will need to sell your services to the employer. Usually people are willing to pay for training out of their own pocket if they are self-employed. If they have an employer, they expect their employer to pay for it.

3. *Can they get information on your topic from other*

sources for less money? The demand for your topic will be limited by the availability of the information you are selling from other sources. There are books, magazines, video cassettes, audio cassettes and adult education classes available everywhere and usually for less than you must charge in order to make a profit.

Don't let this discourage you. Just be aware of it so that you can market your program in such a way that it looks like it's worth the additional cost. The demand for seminars and training programs is increasing in spite of all the other resources available. The reason for this goes back to what we have said earlier. It is not so much what you have to offer or how you present it but it's the way you market and promote your program that determines its success or failure.

If marketed properly the potential participants will perceive that your program would be the best possible way for them to absorb the subject matter in the shortest possible time. In their mind your program would be cost effective. If it appears to be more convenient to obtain the same material from another source at a lower price they will most likely choose the other source.

Many people are uncomfortable in a seminar setting and find that driving to the seminar or workshop and spending a certain amount of time sitting in a room listening to a speaker is less desirable than reading a book or listening to tape cassettes. You are not interested in reaching these people. It just helps to know that there are those who have this point of view.

There are also seminar groupies. They attend every seminar that comes to town. You will get your share of these people too. Generally they are there for entertainment. Whatever a person's reason is for attending your program, you want to target your advertising, promotion and marketing to reach these people.

MARKETING AND PROMOTION

The speaking and seminar business is a promotional sensitive business. Your success will be determined by developing a marketing plan that can be tested and modified inexpensively. I can't tell you how many excellent programs have failed because the speaker or promoter knew little or nothing about marketing and promotion.

Your marketing strategy should be based on your test marketing experience. It is essential to expand what works and quickly get off what doesn't work. Keep in mind that no matter how thorough you are and how much you research your marketing techniques, there will be times when your promotions will fail. Don't let this discourage you. Some of the largest companies in the world with unlimited funds, marketing information, and management experience still have failures from time to time. Through test marketing you will not be put out of business because of one faulty ad, brochure, or media promotion. It will soon become clear what works and what doesn't.

Remember, *two-thirds of your acquisition costs will be for marketing*. This includes promotional design, copyrighting, telephone marketing, media costs, mailing expenses, advertising, etc. A successful promoter can save thousands of dollars in these expenses by focusing on his market from the very beginning. *A mistake many speakers make in the beginning is they select an interesting and needed subject but have no identifiable or reachable audience*. The key is to find a group of people (your market) which you can reach at a reasonable cost.

THE TWO BEST METHODS
TO PROMOTE
YOUR SEMINAR OR WORKSHOP

1. *The one-step promotion cycle.* This type of promotion is usually used in securing a contract with a captive or in-house audience. Basically you convince your client through your promotional material to hire you to present your program to a captive audience such as a sales organization, large corporation, business or association. You sell them on the idea that your presentation will produce a specific benefit or solve a particular problem facing the organization enabling them to be more efficient or make more money in their respective field. You outline the cost of your presentation versus the benefits they will receive as a result of your presentation so that they will want to sign a contract for your services. The one step promotion cycle is usually initiated through direct mail or personal contact.

2. *The two-step promotion cycle.* This is frequently used in investment, real estate and expensive self-

improvement seminars. Basically it works this way: the public is invited to a free lecture on a particular subject. While the free lecture is generally informative, the main purpose is to sell the prospective participant on future seminar, workshop or training programs which will be given for an additional specified fee. The fee can range from $25.00 to $1000.00.

This method is highly successful if the person giving the free lecture is a dynamic, motivational speaker who can turn on the audience and convince them to make an additional investment into a longer, more expensive program. The success or failure of the two-step has a great deal to do with the presenter's personality and ability to win over his audience.

You may not be the type of individual suited to the two-step promotion cycle. Many people are not comfortable with high pressure selling. The two-step doesn't necessarily have to be high pressure but your purpose is to sell the prospective participant your program. You can use a low key presentation but at some point you will have to motivate the prospective participants to take *action*. If you have the type of personality that is more comfortable using a rational sophisticated approach, you will probably have difficulty using the two-step promotion cycle.

Unfortunately most people do not spend their money on a logical rational sales presentation alone. A person's choice to buy is often based on an emotional as well as a rational decision. I know speakers who have had excellent programs and tried to sell their audience with a low key rational approach and failed. If you are not a forceful motivator who can arouse excitement and emotion in your audience, the two-step strategy may not be for you. On the other hand if you are excited about what you do and are committed to your subject matter, you can usually channel that excitement and commitment into a powerful, convincing presentation. It may take a while to develop but I believe anyone can do it if they have the desire.

Something else to consider in using the two-step promotion cycle is that this strategy depends on the quality of the audience you have generated for your free lecture. Questions that must be considered are, *"Can they afford the cost of your program? Are they willing to invest their time in a longer session? and Is your free presentation powerful enough to convince them to take action to invest their time and money based on what you have told them?"*

In my opinion the two-step promotion is one of the most successful methods to promote yourself in the beginning stages of your speaking career. When I first started in the speaking business nearly 12 years ago, I had no experience, training or references. I put together a program and made up my own ads and brochures based on the knowledge I had at that time. My limited budget and experience forced me to be creative in marketing and promoting myself. The obvious choice for me was to use the two-step promotion cycle.

I placed ads in the Wednesday morning and Sunday morning edition of the local paper. My ads were usually 2 columns by 10 inches. I had read somewhere that small ads are a waste of money and are less cost effective. I was right about that. My ads were large enough to get attention. The ad included a brief biography, my photo and some of the points I would cover such as prosperity, problem solving, creative thinking, using your intuition, etc. The prospective participant would be able to learn about these subjects during the free lecture. I even offered a *free gift* for the first 100 people that came to the lecture. This was a two page typed monograph on "How To Make Your Mind A Money Magnet." Everyone is interested in money.

The free lecture was given on Sunday evening at a centrally located hotel. I offered two lectures. One at 6:30 PM and one at 8:00. The same lecture was repeated at both sessions. I learned this trick from my mentor, Anthony Norvell. The hotel charges you for the room for a specific time period. Since I had paid for the room for the evening, it would cost no more to use it twice. This enables you to attract the "early birds" and the "late night" crowd, all in the same evening.

It took a few attempts to refine my marketing and promotion. I tested different ad copy and promotional gimmicks until I found the method that produced the best possible results for the dollars I had to spend. After a short time I was able to attract 200–800 for both free lectures. Out of that audience I signed up 35–40% of those attending the free lecture for a two night seminar given on Monday and Tuesday evening from 7:00–10:00 PM for which I charged $20.00. (This was 10 years ago.) My acquisition cost was about $5.00 per person. (Number of people attending the seminar divided by expenses.) I received a net profit of $15.00 per person plus the income from the sale of my products. Not bad for someone that didn't have any experience.

I have to tell you that there were times when my plan fell on its face. If it rained or there was bad weather the night of the free lecture, practically no one showed up! I still had to go through with the plan but there were times I was lucky to break even and there were times I lost money. However, taking that into consideration I still earned a good living working with the percentages.

If it were not for the two-step promotion cycle, I would not be in business today. It enabled me to market myself without having extensive experience and gave me an opportunity to earn money while I refined my marketing techniques and program material and provided me with referrals that enabled me to start doing in-house programs to sales organizations, companies and associations. Individuals from various companies and organizations attended my public programs and asked me to work with their companies. I was asked if I would speak to their organization on a fee basis. This is how I received my first paid speaking engagement. I did a half hour presentation and was paid $100.00. As a result I was asked back to do a full day seminar. This is how I started doing professional speaking engagements for associations, companies, businesses and various organizations. You can do the same if you are willing to develop and use the two-step promotion cycle.

DIRECT MAIL MARKETING

Direct mail is one of the most expensive ways of marketing your program or services. Using this approach however, you can reach a carefully targeted market not possible with newspaper, radio or TV advertising. With direct mail marketing you can carefully select the audience that will be exposed to your advertisement. Unlike radio, TV or newspaper you are paying only for those people who would most likely be interested in your services.

Direct mail is highly effective because you can specifically target your audience by occupation, income level, profession, common interest or those who have a known history of purchasing products or services similar to yours. The nice part about direct mail is you can accurately reach the clientele to whom you wish to promote your program. Once you have identified the type of individual you wish to reach you can purchase selected mailing lists that closely fit the characteristics of your potential prospects.

The bible for the direct mail industry is DIRECT MAIL LISTS RATES AND DATA. This is published by: *Standard Rates & Data, 5201 Old Orchard Rd., Skokie, Ill. 60067.* Standard Rates & Data provides you with over 20,000 mailing lists you can rent from $20 per thousand up to $100 per thousand names. The average is about $35 per thousand names.

Standard Rates & Data breaks their lists down in the following manner:

1. From whom you can rent the list.
2. Source of the list. Name of the magazine, company, association group the list was obtained from.
3. Rental rates. This would be the cost per thousand names.
4. The minimum number of names you must rent.
5. How the labels are addressed. This tells you the labeling system used.
6. How often the list is updated and maintained. This refers to how often the list is "cleaned."
7. Miscellaneous information relevant to the list.

Most major libraries have a copy of Standard Rates in their reference department. You may want to check there first to get an idea if the Standard Rates and Data is suitable for your purposes. If you are going to use direct mail on a continuing basis it will be an indispensible item.

A 20% discount on list rental is given to "list brokers." You can establish your own list brokerage agency to save this commission but I do not advise it. Granted, many people are doing this successfully but in the long run you will lose out. A competent list broker can save you thousands of dollars. He can help you target your market for the best possible response. He has experience in dealing with various lists and will share his knowledge with you for a 20% commission paid by the list owner.

He will work hard for his 20%. A broker will sit down with you and ask you the right questions in order to effectively produce the list that will target the audience you are seeking to reach. He can provide services and suggestions you may not be aware are available to you. A good list broker is like a good travel agent. He is working for you while getting paid by someone else. He knows that without you he wouldn't have a job so he is anxious to help you reach your objectives.

A good broker wants to develop repeat business. If you are satisfied you will deal with him on a continuing basis. Use his services. You won't be sorry. You can look up list brokers in the yellow pages under Mailing Lists. Most list brokers are reliable so selecting one shouldn't be a problem.

After selecting your list you should put together your brochure or mailing piece. (More on this later.) Make sure your mailing piece reaches the hands of your prospective prospect well in advance of your presentation. As a rule of thumb your brochure should reach your prospective client *3 weeks* before the date of a *local* program. In certain cases your mailing piece should reach them 8 weeks in advance in order to give them time to schedule your program. This is true of people having to travel long distances from out-of-state or individuals who have busy schedules such as doctors or attorneys.

Most of the time you will be using bulk rate because it is much cheaper than first class. The problem with bulk mail is that it is classified as low priority mail and your mailing piece can take a few days or a few weeks to arrive at its destination. Factors affecting this are time of month, time of the year, volume of mail, and the distance your mail will be traveling.

Check with the post office and try to get an idea of what their situation is concerning the various factors mentioned above. You will be surprised how helpful they can be if approached in a cordial and positive manner. Aside from negative remarks we often hear about the postal service employees they are, for the most part, doing an outstanding job. I have found them more willing to go out of their way to help me when I have a question or a problem. Give them a chance to help you and they will.

Generally the return rate for direct mail is from ¾ of 1% to 5% of the entire mailing. A 1% or a 1½% is a good response. Your rate of response will be more with a lower cost product or service than with a more expensive offer. If you are charging higher fees you don't need as large of a response. I like to keep my fees as low as possible in order to afford more people the opportunity to attend my programs. It puts a little more pressure on me because I need more registrants to meet expenses. In the long run I have found it to be profitable because I sell more products and build a larger aftermarket.

We are back to the principle of test marketing again. Never send out a large volume of direct mail without test marketing your list and mailing piece first. An acceptable amount of mailing pieces necessary for testing would be 3000–4000. If you mail 3000–4000 pieces, you can be reasonably sure that you will receive the same response from a larger volume based on the response you received from the initial mailing.

If you mail 3000 pieces to *one list* and receive a 1% response most likely you will receive a 1% response if you mail to 10,000 or 50,000 names on the *same* list. Your test market 3000–4000 names must be done for *each* list you use. In other words, if you use two lists, you have to send out two mailings to determine which list produces a better response. Again, direct mail is one of the best ways to target your audience.

Newspapers and magazines can be one of the most cost effective ways you can promote your seminars and workshops. To use this effectively you must understand the economics of each media and the demographics of their readers.

Standard Rates & Data, Skokie, Illinois publishes four reference guides that are very useful in selecting and working with the media. They are:

1. Newspaper Rates & Data
2. Consumer Magazine Rates & Data
3. Business Publications Rates & Data
4. Newspaper Circulation Analysis

These publications will provide you with the following information:

A. Advertising rates and charges
B. Circulation
C. Editorial profile
D. Representatives and their branch offices
E. Deadline for copy submission
F. Ad sizes and column widths

Their publication *Newspaper Circulation Analysis* is especially helpful if you are going to use the newspaper to promote your program. It will enable you to identify the paper that has the highest readership in the locale of your program *by the people you are seeking to reach*. If you carefully research the material provided in Newspaper Rates and Data you can reach your targeted market at the lowest possible cost.

Never assume that just because a newspaper has a large circulation it will be read by the people you are trying to reach. This is a big mistake many beginners make. You will discover that some of the smaller local papers will draw a larger audience if you check out the demographics first.

A word here about magazines. I don't recommend them for seminar or workshop promotion. In most cases their lead time is too long and their rates are too high to be cost effective. Lead time for magazines is approximately two months which means you will have to tie up your advertising dollars for that period without knowing if your ad is going to produce positive or negative results. If you use newspapers you will know within 4–6 days if your ad pulls. Display ads are the most cost effective way to promote your seminar or workshop. Your ad must present enough information so that the potential participant will be motivated to attend your program or contact you for further information. The two-step works very well in conjunction with newspaper display ads.

If you wish to have the greatest impact with your display ad it would be a good idea to have it prepared by a professional. There are numerous factors involved that will determine the success or failure of a display ad. If you leave it up to the newspaper to prepare your ad it may not turn out the way you want it to. It is always a good idea to have your ad camera ready just the way you want it to appear. Keep in mind that *newspapers pay minimal attention to design and preparation*. A properly prepared display ad can mean the difference between an ad that pulls and one that gets little attention.

One of the best ways to design your ad is to look at similar ads. Check the Sunday paper and notice how other seminar promoters are presenting their ads. Most of their ads have been tested and time proven. Style your ad in a similar fashion. There is no need to reinvent the wheel!

Most newspapers will not guarantee placement of your ad as far as position is concerned. They will do their best to meet your requirements but don't count on it. In the speaking and seminar business it's always wise to keep Murphy's Law in mind, "If something can go wrong, it will!" Double check everything. If you work with an advertising representative it will increase your chances of successful placement. They know the media and are familiar with working with newspapers on a regular basis. It doesn't cost you any more to use advertising representatives. Their fee is paid by the commission they receive from the newspaper for the placement of your ad.

Notice how I continually encourage you to use professional services. Some of these services cost you nothing because the representatives are paid by commission. Some of them will cost you extra dollars in the beginning. This may pose a problem when you are getting started because of a limited budget. However, it has been my experience that professional advice is always less expensive in the long run. Use as much of it as you can so you can concentrate your energies on what you do best, which is speaking! If you work on gaining mastery in your own craft you will have enough money to pay others to do the things you are not familiar with. In the process you will learn from them and be able to do it yourself in the future.

The following is a suggestion of the best possible position for the placement of your display advertising:

1. *Main Section or Main News*. This section is the most read section of the paper. It is especially useful if your program is designed for the general public.
2. *Currents or Lifestyles*. This section is useful if you are appealing to a predominately female audience.
3. *Sports Section*. This section is useful if you are appealing to a predominately male audience.
4. *Economy or Business Section*. This section reaches the high income market. It's especially useful for promoting business, real estate, management and investing seminars.

My experience has been that the larger your ad is and the more often you run it the more people you will attract. Common sense dictates that a balance must be achieved. If you spend $10,000 for ads and take in $5,000 you have to find out what your break even point is so your income exceeds your expenses. Experimenting will tell you how many ads to place before you get to the point of diminishing returns.

If you are going to use a two-step with a free lecture and a program to follow I would suggest *Wednesday morning*, *Thursday morning and Sunday morning*. This has worked out best for me. Over the years I have placed hundreds of ads and based on my experience the best days of the week to advertise seminars and workshops in the *Newspaper* are:

1. Sunday morning
2. Wednesday morning
3. Tuesday morning
4. Thursday morning
5. Monday morning
6. Saturday morning
7. Friday morning

The above are all *morning* editions. The readership for the morning editions for most major cities exceeds the evening edition. If you have a limited budget, use only the morning editions. If you have some extra dollars to spend, you might want to experiment with one or two editions.

THE BEST MONTHS OF THE YEAR TO PROMOTE SEMINARS AND WORKSHOPS ARE AS FOLLOWS:

1. September
2. January
3. April
4. March
5. February
6. October
7. May
8. June
9. November
10. December
11. August
12. July

The days and months can vary according to location and subject matter but in most cases the above days of the week and months of the year are the best time to advertise your program.

PREPARING YOUR BROCHURE

Most small companies, sales organizations, real estate offices etc. receive 60 to 100 direct mail promotional brochures *each week*! The majority of them are thrown into the trash before they are even read. It is estimated that 90% of all direct mail pieces do not get opened by the recipient. It becomes obvious that the first obstacle you must overcome when sending out your promotional mailing piece is *to get the recipient to open your envelope or folder.*

In the speaking and seminar business I have found that a *self mailer* works best. A self mailer is a direct mail piece that requires no envelope. Aside from the fact that it saves a considerable amount of money by eliminating the purchase, stuffing and sealing of the envelope it presents your offer to the recipients for *immediate consideration*. The addressee's name is imprinted on the mailing piece along with the postage permit number. The self mailer eliminates the first obstacle in using direct mail and that is get them to open the envelope.

The next thing to keep in mind is that your maling piece must immediately capture your reader's attention. The *first thing* your potential prospect must be drawn to should be the *most important statement* on your brochure. Then his eye must follow to the next most important statement and the third etc. Before he knows it he is thoroughly involved in reading your entire brochure. To do this your graphic design should control and direct the attention of your potential prospect.

The most effective brochure is one that sells *benefits*. Your brochure should emphasize the benefits your perspective client will gain from your speaking services or seminar. Keep in mind that facts alone won't sell most individuals. There must be a balance between rational facts and the emotional appeal. You must appeal to their logic and emotion. Show them the advantages they will gain from participating in your program. Continue to repeat the *benefits*, both emotional and logical, throughout the brochure. An example of emotional benefits would be happier, have more self-confidence, win people over, be more respected or admired in their community, etc. The logical or rational benefits would be to learn a skill, make more money, increase the size of their business, sell more products or services, etc.

When you write your ad think of yourself as the reader not the person selling the product or service. If you

were the reader of your brochure what benefits would
you want to gain from the product or service being
offered? Learn to be benefit oriented. The primary
question that must be answered before you present
any additional information about who you are or what
you do is "What can this do for me?" If you do not
do this at the onset you will lose your reader immediately. Be simple, clear and specific. The old adage
of K.I.S.S. applies here. (Keep It Simple Stupid!)
Keep in mind you may be thoroughly familiar with
your subject matter but your reader may know little
or nothing about your subject. Educate but don't com-
plicate.

Your message must be clear, concise and comprehen-
sible in *one* reading. To do this keep your brochure
visually appealing and enlightening. A good photo of
yourself will help assure the reader that you are a real
person! It helps him to relax and become more familiar
with you.

We're living in a visually oriented society and photo-
graphs and graphics help to produce a more powerful
message than just your ad copy. As a child you were
trained in school to focus your attention on the printing
under a photograph before reading the rest of the page.
This is a basic teaching method used in textbooks.
Keeping in mind that it is important to give your
strongest promotional message just below your picture
or any other photograph you use on your brochure.
This is an excellent place to emphasize the benefits
of your program or speech.

There are numerous sources of professional services available to help you prepare your ads and brochures. If you do not have a natural ability for copywriting and graphics, I strongly suggest you work with a professional. Again, it will cost you more money initially but in the long run it will pay for itself many times over. I would caution you though to shop around for prices. First check out the quality of work the graphic artist or advertising agency has done for other clients. Next compare his or her price with similar quality work. The advertising, graphic, and typesetting business is price sensitive and the same service from one source can cost three or four times as much from another source. This is particularly true of the printing industry. If you shop carefully and compare quality you can save a considerable amount of money.

Test market your ad and brochure to see if it accomplishes your objective. If it does not draw enough business or has a low pulling power, change part or all of your brochure to increase its efficiency. You may have to seek another professional source to help you discover what needs to be corrected or changed. Once you have refined your brochure you can use it for several years with only minor adjustments. Reader response to your brochure can only be determined by experimenting and testing.

The size and color of your brochure is important. A smaller brochure is best because it is less expensive to produce. If you can keep your brochure to 8½ × 11 you will save a considerable amount of money in printing costs because this is a standard size format that requires no trimming or special stock. The 8½ × 11 format can be folded in numerous ways to change its appearance and appeal. People tend to read and keep a smaller brochure longer. Different colored inks and colored papers will add an appearance of quality to your brochure. Colors are a science in themselves. A competent printer or graphic artist can help you choose the right colors once they are familiar with your material and the type of audience you are trying to reach.

Many brochures use testimonials. Personally, I seldom read testimonials. However, they can be very effective. Most of the ads you see on T.V. for soap powder, coffee, etc., use testimonials. Some people believe them and others think they are pure horse puckey. Sometimes they can work for you by adding to your credibility because the reader has never heard of you before. The most effective testimonials you can use are from individuals or organizations that are familiar to your reader. They add an element of reassurance to an otherwise skeptical or indecisive potential client. If you have some extra space on your brochure you can use this efficiently by including testimonials from sources unknown to your reader. If you have testimonials from famous people or organizations I would suggest you make definite use of them on your brochure. The identification factor will work in your favor.

Your brochure and advertising should contain the following information:

1. *Benefits* ... What benefits will the reader receive

if he or she hires you as a speaker or participates in your program?

2. *Costs* . . . How much will it cost?

3. *Registration or Sign-up procedure.* What do they have to do to sign up for your program or speech?

4. *Payment* . . . What form of payment will you accept? What credit cards can they use? What is your policy on accepting personal checks?

5. *Where can the prospective client contact you?* It is important to put your address in at least two places on your brochure. The most obvious place is the registration form. The other place can be anywhere else on your brochure that blends in graphically. The reason for this is if the registration form is missing from the brochure and someone else receives your brochure they would be able to contact you.

6. *Background Information.* This includes your biography, credentials, and a high quality photo with sharp contrast.

7. *What materials are included with your program or speech?* Will you be handing out any written materials that the participant can expect to receive at your seminar or speech? Also what materials will the participant have to supply?

8. *What options does the participant have if he cannot attend?* Can he purchase your speech or seminar on tape? Will you be presenting another program in his

area that he can attend if he can't attend this one? It's important to give him some options because he may want to participate in the speech, seminar or training program you are offering but may not be able to attend the dates you are promoting.

9. *How can he reply?* This could be a business reply card, envelope, toll free number or a local telephone number. Make it easy for him to contact you.

10. *An Act-Now Motivation.* Provide a reason for the potential client to *act now* before putting away your brochure or advertisement. You can use a free gift or a discount for early registration.

11. *Testimonials.* We discussed this earlier. Use them if they are appropriate.

12. *Tax Deductible Savings.* Include the following statement: "An income tax deduction may be allowed for educational expenses undertaken to maintain or improve professional skills. This includes registration, travel, meals, and lodging. (See Treasury regulation 1.162.5)"

13. *Money back guarantee or refund policy.* Clearly state up front what your policy is on refunding money or guaranteeing satisfaction with your speech or program. The fastest way to ruin your speaking and seminar business is to present speeches and seminars that do not live up to the promises made in your brochure or advertising. A mediocre, low quality, or substandard presentation will catch up with you very shortly and put you out of business. Do not advertise or pro-

mote more than you can deliver. On the other hand, play up the good qualities and benefits of your speech or seminar that you know you can deliver.

USING SPONSORS

A sponsor is an organization which offers your presentation under their auspices. They can add credibility and status to your speech, seminar or workshop if you are not well known to the audience or market you are trying to develop. If they are a national organization you can tie in with their sponsorship throughout the country as you travel from city to city.

An organization, business, corporation or assocation is interested in sponsoring you if they feel your program will be beneficial to their members and employees. When approaching a potential sponsor keep in mind they will be asking the question "How is your presentation going to help us?" This question must be answered to their satisfaction before they will be convinced to work with you.

Remember to send them your press kit and a demo tape to initiate contact. You should have the name of the highest ranking individual in the organization that would be in charge of making a decision on what speakers and what programs the organization will sponsor. Send your demo tape and press kit to his or her attention. Be prepared to call that person within 7–10 days after you have sent out your material. If you are going to talk to him personally have someone on your staff who is in charge of booking follow up. Again, make it easy for potential clients to work with you. You must initiate action to overcome the tendency of the individual to procrastinate, discard your material or put you off.

There are three ways to work with sponsors. First, you can charge a *flat fee* for your presentation where the sponsor takes all the risk or, you can charge on a *per person basis* for each person that registers with or without a guaranteed minimum. If your fee is determined by attendance make sure you have a say in the promotion and advertising of your event. Work closely with the sponsor to keep down the promotional costs and help him to put forth the best possible advertising strategy. The more you are willing to do for the sponsors the more likely they will book you.

The third way to work with sponsors is to help them to make money as a result of your presentation. I frequently do this with church groups. I offer them a 50–50 split of the tuition after expenses. For example, if they enroll 200 participants at $30.00 per person and my travel, meals, lodging, printing and advertis-

ing expenses are $1000.00 the figures would work
out as follows:

Total Tuition	$6000.00	($30 × 200)
Expenses	1000.00	
Net income	5000.00	
50% to organization	2500.00	
Net profit	$2500.00	

You would have a net profit of $2500.00 *plus* income
from the sale of your product. In some cases the sponsor will want a percentage of your product sales. Again,
this is negotiable.

Using this method, not only are you benefiting the
sponsor through the presentation of your material but
the sponsoring organization is benefiting financially
from your presentation. It's a win-win situation for
everyone. Churches are very receptive to the 50–50
sponsorship approach.

Whatever you agree upon as far as finances, presentation, logistics, etc., make sure you *spell it out
clearly in a written contract*. This will prevent any
misunderstanding at the time of settlement. Clearly
state in your agreement exactly what you are going
to do and what compensation you expect for your
services. Also clearly state what they will receive as
their portion of the agreement.

DEVELOPING
AN EFFECTIVE PROGRAM

There are several things you do to develop an effective seminar, workshop or training program.

1. *Make sure your material is interesting, informative and useful.* In today's marketplace, people want nuts and bolts. They are not interested in theory. They want to know *how to do it*. Seminars that are metaphysical, theoretical, or philosophical were popular in the 70's but we're in the 80's now and people are more interested in *practical training*. We are living in an age of high technology. People are willing to pay for information that will effect a measurable change in their productivity, professional skills, or ability to succeed.

They resent paying for information that wastes their valuable time or has little practical application. *Your ability to survive in the speaking and seminar business will be in proportion to the useful, practical information you are able to deliver to your participants.*

2. *Don't waste their time.* Learn to arrange your presentation in such a way as to deliver it in the shortest possible time. The seminars, speeches, workshops and training programs of the 80's will attract people who wish to learn the subject matter as thoroughly as possible in the shortest possible time.

3. *Be entertaining as well as informative.* Humor is the most effective teaching tool available. If you don't have a good sense of humor *you can develop it*. If you already have one, use it! When I started in the speaking and seminar business I was very serious. After all this is serious business! It is easy to take on the characteristics and personality traits of your contemporaries so you can look like, talk like, and act like the person you think you are supposed to be. Like so many people in my profession, I developed a serious, concerned one upmanship "act." When I found out what my Ph.D. really meant (Piled High and Deep), I started to develop a sense of humor. My program participants often tell me that my sense of humor is what made the program one of the most interesting, informative, and memorable programs they have ever attended.

Consider making a lifelong study of humor. Look for it everywhere and integrate it in your speeches and training programs. It will not only enhance your program and help you to become a more effective speaker but it will add immeasurably to the quality of your own life.

4. *Get your audience involved*. Use question and answer sessions to liven up your presentation. This also includes "hands on" activities. Your intention should always be to keep your audience in the "active mode" instead of the "passive recipient mode." This is done by actively engaging your audience in the learning process. Some speakers think their audience is an empty cup and their job is to fill the cup with more information. Nothing could be further from the truth. Education is a process of "bringing forth" information, not cramming it down their throats. The English word education comes from the Latin word *educare* which means "to draw forth." The function of a speaker should be to help the audience to think for themselves and come to their own conclusions. Share your ideas and let your audience work with those ideas until they become part of their own thinking, feeling, action, and reaction. This is the basic function of any good speaker or teacher. Start to think of yourself as not only a speaker but an *educator*.

5. *Make your audience as comfortable as possible*. There are some speakers and seminar promoters who intentionally try to make the participant as physically uncomfortable as possible. They hold long sessions without stretch breaks and some don't even allow restroom breaks. That's total nonsense. Regularly scheduled breaks will relieve tiredness, restlessness, and boredom. A good technique is to alternate from lecture to audience participation. This will help to keep your audience's interest because each individual responds to different methods of learning.

PROGRAM MATERIALS

Whenever you are going to present a speech, seminar or workshop, have your books, tapes, audio visuals, hand-outs, and other materials ready to ship several weeks prior to your speaking engagement. If you allow enough time for delivery, you can ship your materials less expensively. For books and tapes you can use the special *4th class book rate*. This will save you over 50% of the regular parcel post rate. The best way to ship your other materials is by United Parcel Service. UPS does not give a discount for books and tapes so the 4th class special rate is the most economical.

In some cases you may wish to take your materials with you to the location of your program. Airlines do not charge for the first two items you check in as baggage. For additional items they usually charge $7.00 to $10.00 per item. You can avoid the extra charge if you use a skycap. He will check your additional items for $1.00 or $2.00 per item. If I have 5 items, I check in the first two items at the ticket counter and have the skycap check in the additional 3 items before I enter the terminal. Most of the time they are stationed in front of the terminal.

Make sure to confirm the arrival of any items you have shipped through the Postal Service or UPS. Never assume your packages arrived safely. If they were lost in shipment, you can make arrangements to take your materials with you.

PROGRAM REGISTRATION

It is essential that you have competent help at the registration table if you are presenting a seminar or a workshop. In most cases it would be wise to hire reliable temporary help from an agency located in the city in which you will be speaking. This is less expensive than bringing your own staff. I always contract services from *two different* agencies in the city I am working. By doing this I can be reasonably assured that at least one of them will show up and one of them will be competent enough to handle the assignment.

Handling reservations yourself is tacky and takes away from your credibility as a professional speaker. Hire temporary help to handle this for you and make sure they arrive at least one hour in advance before the scheduled registration so you can show them exactly what to do. Your help at the registration table will create either a positive or negative environment for the initial contact with your participants. It's extremely important to create a favorable image right from the beginning. It sets the tone for the rest of the day.

MISCELLANEOUS REMINDERS
FOR A SUCCESSFUL
SEMINAR OR WORKSHOP

1. Check and recheck your hotel meeting and sleeping rooms reservations.

2. Have extra copies of your presentation materials in case you lose them or they get lost in transit. Have your secretary package a spare copy of everything you will need for your presentation and that package ready for shipping at a moment's notice. If something goes wrong, you can have it shipped by air freight which will put it in your hands within a few hours.

3. Repeat all the participants' questions before answering them. Most people are shy in a group situation and tend to speak softly. This prevents your audience from hearing the question. Help your audience and help your participants by repeating their questions before answering them.

4. *Keep on schedule*. Have enough consideration for your audience to begin on time and end on time. People are busy and will appreciate this courtesy. Also, don't allow the breaks to lag. Set a certain amount of time for each break and then start on time. It is helpful if you ring a bell or flash the lights to let your participants know it's time to start again.

5. *Maintain eye contact with your audience*. Nothing is worse than a speaker who does not look at his audience. Treat every participant as if he or she were the only person attending the program.

6. *Acknowledge all phone and mail registrants*. Send a letter or a post card to every registrant. The card should include an acknowledgement for the money they have sent to you, the date, place, and time of your presentation and if possible, a small map showing the exact location of your meeting.

7. *Use name tags*. This will help the participants to get to know each other and make them feel more welcome. It also serves as a visual indicator of those who have paid. If you hand out the name tags at the registration table after payment has been confirmed you will know if anyone has "slipped in" without paying. Stick-on tags work best because they will not damage the individual's clothing.

8. *Make it easy for your participants to find you*. When your participants arrive at your meeting place, make sure they can find you. On the surface this may seem absurd but I know of several cases where a speaker

was holding a program and the hotel did not have him listed *anywhere*. There were no signs or listing at the front desk, and no listing on the hotel activity board for that day. The participants were turned away because the seminar promoter failed to check this out and make it easy for his participants to find him. Have standard signs with arrows on them and your name imprinted pointing out the way to the room where you will be working.

9. *Have coffee, water, or refreshments*. Once your temporary help signs the participants in, have some coffee, water, or refreshments for them. This will give them something to do before you get started and will help them adjust to their new surroundings.

KNOW YOUR AUDIENCE

If you want to be successful in the speaking and seminar business, it is imperative that you understand the audience with which you will be working. The important question that should be foremost in your mind is "What do they expect to get out of my program or speech?" and "What is their motivation for attending this program?"

Psychology teaches that there are only two reasons for a human being to do anything. The first is to *gain benefits* and the second is to *escape losses*. Your presentation should center on helping the participant to solve one of these two basic needs. The participant's reason for attending your program can be broken down into several factors that encompass these two basic needs:

1. *A desire to learn more about the subject matter.*

The motivation here is *education*. The individual feels that if he can learn the subject matter you are presenting he will benefit in some way.

2. *A desire to earn more money*. The benefit here is increased wealth. Programs that show participants how to earn more money or create more wealth have the highest attendance.

3. *A desire to change an unwanted behavior pattern*. The motivation here is to escape losses. The individual feels if he can learn how to change or get rid of unwanted behavior patterns, he will escape the emotional pain the habit is causing him.

4. *Career change*. The individual feels he will gain knowledge and skills to make necessary career changes either by moving up in his company or changing careers entirely.

5. *Individual or group management*. The individual feels he can gain benefits by learning how to manage his time, business, finances, employees, etc.

6. *Individual is required to take your program*. He is encouraged or obligated to take your program through his employer, trade, or profession. The sponsoring organization usually pays for the training and requires the individual to attend. In this case the individual's motivation is to escape losses (disapproval from the sponsoring organization) and to gain benefits. (To learn the subject matter you will be presenting.)

HOW TO HANDLE
A DISSATISFIED PARTICIPANT

Occasionally you will encounter an individual who is dissatisfied with your presentation. It helps to have a policy prepared in advance as to how you are going to handle these situations. Before you begin your presentation, briefly restate your policy and then stick to it. Don't change it with each individual situation. Treat everyone the same. Once the participants know the rules, they will comply with relatively little trouble. Most of the confusion comes from people not knowing your policy in advance.

I have a standard money back guarantee. If a participant is dissatisfied in any way, I will refund his money right on the spot. I do not want their money if I cannot satisfy their reason for attending. My only stipulation is that they must stay for the entire program. This eliminates making judgments about the program before they have heard the entire presentation. If at that point they feel they have not received full value for their money, I am more than willing to refund their money. This policy is clearly stated up front.

In the 12 years I have been doing programs I have had very few people avail themselves of this guarantee. A money back policy is assuring to the skeptic or individual who is not a risk taker. Your money back guarantee will put the participant at ease and allow him to fully participate in your program without worrying if he made the right decision. I want to reemphasize that whatever policy you decide to follow, be consistent with it and stick to it.

ANSWERING QUESTIONS

I believe most participants have legitimate questions that should be answered. However, in every audience there are one or two individuals who want to hold their own seminar with your audience. Perhaps they are frustrated speakers who are upset because you're booked and they aren't. More than likely they are individuals who receive very little attention and recognition at home or at work; perhaps they feel the ideal way to get the attention they think they deserve is to use your audience as a forum for airing their viewpoints.

There are also individuals who will ask questions that are entirely out of context or ask questions that will interrupt the flow of ideas you are presenting at that moment. If you acknowledge the question you do not have to answer it at that moment. You can say "I will cover that in a few moments or later on. If I don't, please bring it up again." If it's a quick question that will not interrupt the flow of your presentation, it is best to answer it right away.

It is important to keep a balance between participation and control. You want your participants to have an active role but you don't want them to control the program. I have given my presentation hundreds of times so I can usually anticipate questions and answer them before they are asked. This eliminates the obvious questions and allows the program to move along at a smooth and rapid pace.

Be aware of individuals who are trying to "set you up." They are constantly looking for ways to "catch" you so you look bad and they look good. Their game is to ask questions to "trap" you to see if you really know what you are talking about. This type of individual wastes time, bores the rest of the audience, and creates an uncomfortable environment. It takes time to develop skill in turning off these individuals without embarrassing them.

The two most effective ways I have found to handle this are to give short answers and then without stopping, continue on with your presentation or tell them to see you at the break and you will answer their question in detail. The point here is you want to encourage audience participation but always keep the presentation under your leadership and control.

TAPE RECORDING
YOUR PRESENTATION

Never, never allow your presentation to be recorded. Have a firm policy on this. Make sure it is included as part of your contract. The reason for this is obvious. You want to sell your own recordings. A less obvious reason is that the clicking and tape changing from the recorders is distracting to you and your audience.

I inform my audience at the beginning of my presentation that there is no tape recording but that professionally recorded material will be available later in the day. This is standard procedure for most speakers. You don't have to dwell on the subject. Mention it briefly and move on.

You can eliminate most recorders entirely by having "NO TAPE RECORDINGS" signs printed in advance. Take some with you to each presentation and put them by the registration table. I instruct my staff at the registration table to encourage the participants who are carrying tape recorders to return to their automobile and leave the recorders there so they will not lose them or forget them when they leave. If this is handled tactfully, most people will comply without question.

SELECTING AND RENTING
MEETING ROOMS

SELECTING AND RENTING
MEETING ROOMS

Nothing does more to enhance or detract from your image than your selection of your meeting facility. This is an area where you would not cut back on expenses. Always pick a first class, high quality, meeting facility.

The first priority in choosing your meeting facility is *location*. Is it easily accessible and is it central? People do not like to travel across town to attend a seminar nor do they want to go to a place that does not have ample parking. Accessibility to a freeway is a prime consideration in choosing your meeting site.

Don't forget the safety factor. This is especially true if your program is for women. Most likely they will be arriving and leaving alone at night. If the facility you have chosen is located in a high crime area, participants, especially women, will hesitate to attend.

Try to find a hotel or meeting facility with a well-lit parking area, in a low crime area with a restaurant or coffee shop on the premises.

Choosing a hotel in an unfamiliar area can be a problem. It would be wise to pick up a copy of a hotel guide that has some sort of rating system. You can use the AAA guide or ask your travel agent to help you choose a hotel. They usually have hotel guides with a rating system. If the guide uses a five star rating system never choose a hotel that has less than a four star rating.

You must also be aware that some hotel chains have more than one hotel in the same city. This can be confusing to the participant as to which hotel is the right hotel. I have given programs in some cities where there were several hotels with the same name and some of them were on the same street! Eliminate this if you can.

Your best bet is to ask around and find out what the best facility is in town. This is the one you should try to book. One of the ways you can do this is to notice what hotels other promoters are using. If different promoters keep using the same hotel, you can be confident enough that it will be suitable for your activity.

The national hotel chains usually have a toll free number you can call to book any one of their hotels throughout the country. This is convenient but I do not recommend it for booking a meeting room. It has been my experience that negotiating directly with the hotel I plan to use produces the best results. The hotel sales and catering departments can be very helpful in planning your activity and often can save you a considerable amount of money by offering you options that may not be available if you are arranging services through a central toll free operator.

When dealing with the sales and catering department, keep in mind that they prefer to sell sleeping rooms with catered meals. They are most likely to give preference to a client that wants to book large blocks of sleeping rooms, meals and meeting rooms. The lowest priority are meeting rooms without meals or lodging. If your activity falls in this category, understand that you will not be given the highest priority.

BOOKING YOUR SLEEPING ROOM

Let the sales or catering staff book your sleeping room for you. Most of the time you will end up getting a better room at a lower rate than if you booked the room yourself. They usually provide a lower business or corporate rate because they are aware that you will be using their meeting and/or catering services.

THE BEST STRATEGY FOR BOOKING YOUR MEETING FACILITIES

1. *Deal directly with the hotel you wish to book*. Avoid the national sales office or toll-free reservation.

2. *Contact the sales or catering office when you make your meeting room reservation*. Your initial contact should be by phone. If you call them you will get much better results. After you have made arrangements by phone, always ask for a written confirmation of everything you discussed on the phone.

3. *Request less space than you need*. If I want a room that will accommodate 100 people I will ask for a room for 75. The reason for this is that it will usually be the same room. If you ask for a room for 100 people they may charge you $125.00. If you ask for a room that holds 75 people they will probably charge you $80.00.

Ask them how many people the room will hold. If it will hold a maximum of 75 people, then you will have to negotiate for a larger room. If they say they have a room that holds 100–150 then tell them you need it for 75. If they say the room only holds 75 tell them you don't want to crowd everyone in. If they have the space and it isn't booked, they will usually put you in a larger room for the same price.

Generally most hotels do not have a set rate. Their staff is trained to get as much as the traffic will bear. Always negotiate with them and never take their first offer. Once they are aware you know what the game is, they will get serious and negotiate with you to secure your business. After a few negotiations, you will become an expert at booking your meeting facilities.

4. *Check arrangements when you arrive*. Double check everything when you first arrive. Murphy's Law applies here! It's a very rare occasion when the accommodations will be exactly to the specifications you agreed upon with the hotel. I try to arrive one day in advance to solve the potential logistic problems. Make up your mind that you will probably have to take charge of handling most things yourself. This doesn't seem fair since you are paying for services but it's a fact of life in dealing with hotels. Don't assume that careful communications, a signed agreement, and clarity on your part will eliminate misunderstandings. Be prepared.

SEATING ARRANGEMENTS

The seating arrangements you select will influence the cost of the room. The least expensive is theater style. Most meeting rooms are set up theater style where the chairs are arranged in rows. School room style is where you will be using tables or desks. As a general rule school room style will hold about half the people theater style will.

I have found that most people are comfortable with theater style. If considerable note taking or writing exercises will take place, I book the room for school room style. To avoid the additional expense of school room style, I encourage participants to bring a bound notebook with a hard cover to the seminar. This gives them something to write on without needing a desk or a table.

AUDIO VISUAL

Most hotels do not have their own audio visual equipment. Their equipment is ordered on a rental basis from a local company and the cost is passed on to you. Lately the hotels have been charging for every item of equipment you use. Today they even charge an additional fee for a chalkboard (and chalk) which in the past was always included with the room. Again, know in advance what you will be needing and what they will charge you for the use of the equipment. If you do not bring your own audio visual equipment make sure you test the equipment you have ordered *before* your program begins. Do this as far in advance of your meeting as you can.

SERVING COFFEE

Coffee is a pain in the a--! It's expensive and it's the number one rip-off in dealing with hotels. Your participants appreciate having coffee and the hotel loves it because they make a killing on the price they charge you!

Generally the hotels charge you by the cup. The price can range anywhere between 60¢ to $1.00 per cup! You can lower the cost and save a considerable amount of money if you make arrangements with the hotel to purchase your coffee by the gallon instead of the cup. Most of the time you can save 40% or more over the cup price. The hotels don't like to do this but they will if they have no other choice.

If the hotel provides large cups, which is another gimmick, ask them to bring smaller cups. If you use a 5 oz cup instead of an 8 oz or a 10 oz cup, your coffee will go much further and you will discourage waste.

If there is some coffee left over after your coffee break, don't let the hotel take it back. When they bring a new batch of coffee for the next break, they will be selling you the same coffee again! Insist that the remaining coffee stay in the room until the container is empty.

If you are considering providing pastry there is one piece of advice I can share with you . . . FORGET IT! It's a waste of money and most people will be just as happy with coffee.

IN-HOUSE MEALS

At some seminars it is advantageous to include the cost of lunch in your registration fee. I frequently do this when there will be 300 or more participants for a full day seminar. With that many people it's very difficult for all of them to find a restaurant and be back in time for the afternoon session. There is an advantage in ordering a meal because the hotel will waive or substantially reduce the cost of the meeting room rental fee if you purchase meals.

There are also disadvantages to consider. Providing meals is one extra item you must plan, make arrangements for and negotiate. In essence, it is one more thing that can go wrong. In addition to this, you must factor the cost of the meal into your tuition. This makes it appear that your program is more expensive than it would normally be.

There is a certain psychology involved. Most people will have to eat out anyway and will probably pay as much or more for their lunch at a restaurant. If this is the case, they don't think of buying their own lunch as part of the cost of the seminar. Also, if they don't like the meal the hotel serves the tendency is to have less than positive feelings for the rest of the day. On the other hand, if they buy their own lunch and they don't like it, they most likely will not blame you.

If you do contract for meals make sure you know exactly what the charges will be. This includes set-up, gratuities, taxes, etc. Hotels have a way of escalating the cost of meals through surcharges. They are hesitant to mention these charges when making arrangements. Have them give you an exact quote to the penny for each meal that will be served.

PAYING YOUR BILL

When you have received your bill for the services you have contracted for, check it out very carefully. Hotels are notorious for lack of communication between staff members and are likely to charge you for things you don't order or items that were supposed to be included in the original cost estimate. Example: They may have included a chalkboard for your "convenience" and then bill you $10.00 for it later. You do not have to pay for anything that is not included or spelled out in your contract. That's why it's so important to have everything in writing.

SETTING THE PRICE
FOR YOUR PRESENTATION

Your price should be set at the highest level your participants are willing to pay to attend your program. How can you determine this? The only way to find this out is through testing. It won't take you long to find out what price is appropriate for your program. Once you have determined what the highest price is, I would suggest backing off just a little and set your fee a little lower than most participants are willing to pay. This will help to attract the cost-conscious individual who determines all his decisions based on price.

Other factors involved are operating costs, cost of materials, audio-visuals, promotional costs, clerical support, transportation, hotel room, lodging, etc.

PAYMENT

I know several speakers who use the *advance registration only* system. This guarantees their attendance.
If they do not receive a favorable response, they cancel
their program. They reason that this lowers their risk
of failure. This works for some speakers but I don't
recommend it. I have found that a *combination of
advance registrations at the door* produces the best
results. Granted, you will have no idea of exactly how
many people will sign up but this is offset by increased
registrations. If you offer an incentive for advance
registration, you will have 90% of your participants
preregister. Some people, for various reasons, simply
cannot make a decision in advance. There is no reason
to turn them away if you combine both types of registration.

CHECKS AND CREDIT CARDS

There is a certain amount of risk when accepting personal checks. However, in the speaking and seminar business the risk factor is very low. In most cases it would be to your advantage to accept personal checks. The increase in business will more than offset the few bad checks you will occasionally encounter.

Credit cards are a low risk way of increasing your registrations and product sales. If the amount of purchase is less than $50.00 you usually do not have to have an authorization. This can be overcome by making out more than one charge slip if the purchase is in excess of $50.00.

For years I avoided credit cards because I didn't want to bother to carry around the charge card machine and credit card slips. I thought they were too much bother and if I didn't have charge cards people would find another way to pay. *I was wrong*. A friend of mine convinced me to use credit cards and as a result my registration and product sales income increased 30%. If you are not using them, you're losing money! Don't take my word. Test it for yourself.

BEST MONTHS OF THE YEAR
TO HOLD SEMINARS AND WORKSHOPS

Based on my 12 years of experience in the speaking and seminar business, I have found the following months to be the best months to hold a seminar or workshop:

If the participant is paying the cost:

January
October
September
March
June
April
February
November
May
July
December
August

If the organization is paying the tuition:

March
October
April
November
September
February
January
June
May
August
July
December

BEST DAYS OF THE WEEK
TO HOLD A SEMINAR
OR WORKSHOP:

If the organization is paying the tuition:

Thursday
Wednesday
Tuesday
Friday
Saturday
Monday
Sunday

If the participant is paying for the tuition:

Saturday
Monday
Tuesday
Wednesday
Thursday
Friday
Sunday

FACTORS INVOLVED
IN SCHEDULING YOUR PROGRAM:

1. *Vacation periods*. Attendance drops considerably in July and August.

2. *National holidays*. Especially around Easter, Christmas, and Thanksgiving.

3. *Religious holidays*. A consideration when working with a Jewish group.

4. *Major national events*. Watch out for national elections and major sporting events.

5. *Major local events*. This includes local elections, sports activities and school graduations. June attendance can be affected by school graduations.

6. *Public transportation*. This is a key consideration when working in large metro areas where participants rely heavily on transit systems.

7. *Daylight savings time*. Senior citizens and some younger participants are reluctant to go out at night. If it gets dark early, they may put off attending entirely.

8. *Hotel bookings*. Check and see if there is a convention in town that has most of the hotels booked. This will affect your attendance and logistic problems.

9. *Competition*. Is someone else doing the same type of program at the same time and date? If so, reschedule.

10. *Labor strikes or pending labor strikes*. This is a special concern if the strikers are transit workers or hotel staff.

AWARDING CERTIFICATES

If possible have some sort of certificate printed up to give to your participants upon completion of your program. It will add to your image and credibility and will be an excellent form of public relations for your program. It's good public relations because participants usually frame them and hang them up on the wall. Others will inquire about the program thereby making it an excellent source of referral business.

GETTING STARTED
ON THE "LOCAL CIRCUIT"

One of the best methods to expand your speaking activity is to put your program on the "local circuit," traveling from one *local* city to another. The savings in time and money can be substantial because your travel and advertising budget can be kept at a minimum. You can travel by auto thus eliminating plane fares and transporting materials. Other savings can be had by placing your ad in one newspaper that covers more than one city. Your ad can list the dates, times, and places you will be presenting the same program in each city.

When traveling by auto on the "local circuit," weather is a prime consideration in planning your schedule. In fact, *all* my scheduling is done according to weather patterns. Personally, I don't like cold weather so I book the colder areas in the warmer seasons. Sometimes I drive or rent a car in the area I will be working and travel the cities in a 100 mile area. This can be very cost effective because of the savings in time, travel, and advertising. Booking in warm climates insures that my program won't be cancelled because of ice or snow storms.

Conducting your program on a local level will give you a chance to test your advertising and promotion. It will enable you to refine your program for future markets in other locations on a nationwide basis. This is called "roll out." If your program is successful in small to medium-sized cities and towns, it will probably roll out successfully in most major cities throughout the country.

PREPARING YOUR
INTRODUCTION AND CLOSING

Whenever you speak you should have someone introduce you and close with a brief message. You do not want your introduction or closing to be "off the cuff" or "impromptu." To insure continuity always have a *printed* introduction with you every time you make a presentation.

Take a few moments and coach the person who will be giving your introduction and closing message. Instruct him to please read *only* the printed introduction you have provided and not to add or omit anything. Remind him that your presentation is tied to your introduction and that things will go much more smoothly if he reads it *exactly* as written.

Your introduction should include the following items:

1. A brief biography.

2. Your educational background.
3. Work experience in your field.
4. Some of your accomplishments such as articles you have written for well known magazines and the title of the book(s) you have written.

Your conclusion

When you end your seminar or speech you should have a powerful conclusion. This could be a story or a personal experience that creates a highly emotionally charged feeling in your audience. It can also be something humorous that you have thoroughly tested and you know will arouse laughter and excitement in your audience. You want them to remember you and you want to create good feeling; as a result they will be more receptive to investing in your products which are offered for sale in the back of the room after your presentation.

As your speech or seminar concludes, it's important that the person who introduced you or the one in charge of the closing message be on standby for your "cue." He must be informed in advance of the content of your products rather than the products of several speakers. If the break comes one or two speakers later, this may not be the case.

As you can see, not only is the wording of your introduction and conclusion important, but the timing and placement of your speech on the day's agenda as well. Both contribute to your overall success that particular day. Those assigned to the introductory and closing message want to do a good job for you but you must take the total responsibility for the presentation of a smooth and effective introduction and closing.

PUBLISHING AND MARKETING YOUR OWN BOOKS AND TAPE CASSETTES

To be *financially* successful in the speaking and seminar business, you must have "product." The term "product" in the context of the speaking and seminar business specifically refers to tape cassettes and books. If you do not have a sufficient amount of product to sell at your speeches, seminars, and workshops, you will miss out on a substantial portion of your potential income. The reason for this is that the *majority* of your gross income *will not* come from speaking fees or seminar registrations but rather from the sale of your product. Most speakers, including myself, earn 60% of their income from the sale of their product.

If you are seriously considering making a living as a professional speaker, it is essential that you put together a tape cassette package and offer one or more books for sale. In this section we will discuss how to put together a package that will be attractive, saleable, and financially profitable.

THE MONOGRAPH

When I first started in the speaking and seminar business, I did not have a book. To fill the gap while I was writing my first book, I developed several "monographs." A monograph is 10–20 double-spaced typed pages bound in an attractive cover. The pages are xeroxed or printed on plain white stock and the cover is a heavier weight colored stock with the title of the monograph printed on it.

The printing cost for monographs is very inexpensive in comparison to the cost of printing a book. Based on current printing costs, you should be able to produce 500 monographs for somewhere between $150 to $200. This would include 15 pages with an attractive cover. Each page is printed on one side so you will actually have 15 sheets of paper.

The title of your monograph should correspond with

the subject matter of your speech or seminar. It should not have the exact same material as your presentation but should include additional information or a review of your subject matter. The participants' motivation for purchasing it should be to have more complete or detailed information on your subject matter. If you were giving a seminar on "Prosperity," your monograph could be about a specific way to generate income based on the principles you shared with your participants. You might want to use a title such as "How To Turn Misfortune Into A Fortune!"

Monographs can easily bring $5.00 to $10.00...at point of sale during your seminar, speech or workshop. You couldn't sell them in a bookstore for that price, but at the time of your presentation you have the advantage of being able to create a positive need and desire for the material contained in your monograph. Your printing costs would be less than 50¢ each so you can see the potential for profit is enormous. As I look back, I can see how I made more money on my monographs than I presently make on my published books. Of course I am selling more books, but the per unit profit was considerably higher on the monographs.

The monograph is characterized by:

1. Low printing cost.
2. Ability to print small quantities economically.
3. Fast turnover.
4. Ability to print, publish and market in the shortest possible time.
5. Allows the beginning speaker to have "product" to sell at his or her first speech or seminar.

Remember, before you start speaking professionally, even if it's only on a part-time basis, it is essential that you either write a book or develop a monograph. The monograph will help you to get started while working on your book. In addition to that, it will produce enough income for you to print and publish your first book.

YOUR FIRST BOOK

The next step is to write a book that is related to your subject matter. Your book will not only make money for you but it will add to your credibility, image, and prestige. It will help to characterize you as a professional. Monographs won't add much to your prestige but they will add a great deal to your pocketbook, which is their primary function in the beginning. A book will do both.

If you have never written a book before, don't let that discourage you. It's not as difficult as you may think. If you are thoroughly versed on your subject matter and can speak on the same topic for three or four hours, you can write a book. You may need help with the final writing and editing, but you can do most of the manuscript yourself. When your manuscript is finished you can take it to a professional editor or to an individual who has had some writing experience and they can help you "polish it up."

The best way to write a book is to write *two or three pages a day*, no more, no less. The discipline of doing two or three pages a day, *every day* will enable you to produce your first manuscript within 90 days. This is the least stressful and most productive way I know of to produce a book when you have never written one before. If you sit down and think "Gosh, I have to write a book in 90 days!", you'll become overwhelmed with the project and probably won't get started. Think in terms of two or three pages a day and you will have it done in 90 days without anxiety. Keep in mind you're going to make a lot of money and you're going to be more famous after you write your book.

The next step is to have your book published. At this point I want to tell you that you will be wasting an incredible amount of time and energy looking for a publisher. Especially if you are an "unknown." Only one out of every 10,000 manuscripts received by publishers ever gets into print. You can't afford the odds and you haven't got the time.

You want your book published as soon as possible so you can build your speaking and seminar business. Your book is not only a product that you can sell to increase your income but it's a primary marketing tool that you can use to promote yourself for future booking engagements. Your book will add to your fame, prestige and credibility. You need all three to be successful in the speaking and seminar business.

Once you have decided to go to press it is important that you pick the right book printer. Do not go to a regular printer. Find a company that specializes in short run book printing. You can locate them in the yellow pages under "book printers". I have checked several of them out and found their business ethics to lie somewhere between outright dishonesty to total integrity. The most reliable source for me has been Banta Company. They have the highest degree of integrity, experience, and competence in the book publishing and printing business. They are not a "vanity" publisher. They are a book *printer*. As a printer they can save you a considerable amount of money when printing and publishing your own book. Write to: *Banta Company, Curtis Reed Plaza, Menasha, WI 54592*

When pricing your book you should keep this rule of thumb in mind: the cover price of your book should be *at least* 3 times your printing cost. If it costs $2.00 to print your book you should charge no less than $6.00. If you are going to sell them primarily through your seminars and speaking engagements, you can easily sell them for $7.95.

People will pay more for a book sold at a seminar than they will in the bookstore. I know of many speakers who sell their books for $10.00 or more and have no problem moving large quantities. We're talking about soft cover books here. A hard cover book can bring $15.00 to $30.00. In my opinion it's better to stick to paperbacks. They are easier to handle, sell more rapidly and will produce more income due to volume sales.

Your initial printing costs will be somewhere between $3,000 and $4,000 for a 150 page book. The first printing is more expensive because of the typesetting. You can finance this through the sale of your monographs. Put all the income aside you earn from your monographs and within a short time you have enough money to reinvest in your first book printing.

Now is the time to get started on that book. Two pages today and two pages tomorrow and pretty soon you will have your first book ready for publication. Your book is going to help you become famous and rich. That should be enough motivation to get started today!

IF YOU ARE NOT READY
TO WRITE A BOOK

Being part of an "anthology" is an ideal solution. An anthology is a collection of short chapters or stories in one book. The Royal Publishing Company puts together anthologies for speakers. They will print your chapter as part of a larger book with other successful individuals. There are many advantages to this:

1. Your name will be in good company with people who are successful speakers and seminar leaders.

2. You will be a published author.

3. Your picture, name and address go inside with your chapter.

4. You can buy the anthologies wholesale with custom cover jackets to sell at your speeches and seminars.

For more information on this exciting concept contact: *Royal Publishing Co. 18823 Hicrest Rd., Glendora, Ca. 91740*

TAPE CASSETTES

Tape cassettes have the highest profit margin of any product you can sell as a speaker. They can add thousands of dollars to your gross profits if they are marketed properly. Most speakers offer cassette packages which retail somewhere between $30 to $300. A general rule of thumb is that each cassette should be priced for no less than $10 each.

If you have 4 cassettes you should charge *no less* than $40.00 for your cassette pack. You will probably want to add a few dollars for the album, inserts, labels, etc. A cassette pack of 4 tapes with an album can easily be sold for $45.00. The best part is that it will cost you somewhere between $7.00 and $9.00! As you can see there is a tremendous profit in cassette tapes.

How do you go about putting together your cassette pack? First, you must write your tape scripts. This is similar to writing a book manuscript. The industry average is 20 minutes of recording time on each side of the cassette. This means you will need *eight* 20 minute scripts to produce a 4 cassette package.

You will not need a script if you record your program live. I don't recommend this. In the long run you will lose business because people would rather have your seminar on tape than attend in person, if given a choice. If they do not have to go to the seminar to get the material they are more likely to "borrow" the tapes from a friend. I have found that participants are more likely to "share" their tapes if they are recorded live. One person will take the seminar and pass the tapes on to a friend. If the friend realizes he has to take the training "live" he is more likely to attend. The tapes should be *supportive* material which is based on your subject matter.

After writing your scripts you will need to find a place to record them. *Do not record on your own tape recorder*. The background noise will ruin the quality of your tapes. Find a reliable recording studio. You can look them up in the yellow pages under "recording services". Make sure you shop around for price. Recording studios charge by the hour. You don't need a fancy studio because, most likely, you will not be recording music. In addition to their hourly rate there is an "*editing charge*" and a charge for *tape*. Check all of the above very carefully and have them give you a *complete* estimate. This is a one time expense so get the best possible service for your dollar.

After you have completed your recordings and they are edited the studio will make a master tape. You own this tape and can take it to any tape duplicating service for production. There are numerous tape duplicating services in every major city. Again, check out their prices and services. Ask them for a sample of their work. Once you have narrowed your choice down to the companies you think you would like to work with, your final decision shoud be based on the answers to the following questions:

1. *How fast can you produce my tapes?* What is your turn-around time from the time I place my order to the time I receive delivery?

2. *How many cassettes do I have to buy at a time?* Find out what their minimum order is.

3. *Will you ship them (drop ship) to my speaking and seminar location?* This service will save you a lot of time and reshipping expense.

4. *What kind of packaging do you offer?* This would include shrink wrap, albums, boxes, etc.

5. *What is your charge per tape, per album, etc?* Get an itemized list of their charges per item.

You can have a good quality tape reproduced from your master for about 60¢ to $1.50 each. The right price range would be somewhere in the middle. Don't make the mistake of buying cheap tapes to increase your profits. You will also increase your headaches with returned tapes. Also, don't let them talk you into expensive tapes either. If you are not recording music you do not need to buy the top of the line. If you are recording music, I would suggest using music quality tapes.

Over the years I have worked with dozens of tape duplicating companies. The best value I have found is *Southwest Cassettes, 3470 E. Paradise Dr., Phoenix, Az. 85028.* They have an excellent balance between service quality and price.

SELLING YOUR PRODUCTS

OK, you now have your products ready for sale. How do you sell them to your participants? Before I answer this I want to say something about the *hard sell* that most speakers are using today. I not only think it is unnecessary, but in the long run I believe it will be counterproductive because you will be perceived as a "hustler" and a "peddler." Your reputation will eventually catch up to you and you'll find fewer and fewer organizations wanting to work with you.

The method most speakers use is to keep referring to their tapes and books throughout their presentation. They use inferences such as "There is a lot more in my tapes" or "I can't cover this completely now but it's in my book." Essentially they are using their presentation to create a "need" for their tapes and books. Their justification for this is that the participants will gain benefits from using their materials. While this may be true, I am uncomfortable with this approach.

I firmly believe that if you do an outstanding job with your speech or seminar, you will not have to "sell" your participants on the idea that they need your tapes and books. On the contrary, they will *want* to buy them. Don't misinterpret what I'm saying. You have to *mention* your tapes and books and you have to explain to your audience what they're about, but you don't have to "push" them by using the hard sell.

I find that audiences are more sophisticated today and they're getting tired of being worked over by one speaker after another. If you will concentrate on the *quality of your presentation* and use a *soft sell*, you will have much better results. Give them full value for their money with a quality presentation and they will *insist* on buying your products. They *want* to take you home but they *don't want* to be coerced into taking you home.

With a little experience you can usually depend on selling 30% to 60% of your participants one or more products. Most of the time your income from product sales will be greater than your speaking fee. Perhaps this is why so many speakers use the hard sell. The bottom line is you have to do what works best for you. The information in this section is provided so that you'll be clear on your options.

Whatever you sell, make sure it is packaged attractively. Quality packaging and graphics will go a long way in helping you sell your products. Also, be careful how you hold your books and tapes when referring to them. Don't throw them around. Handle them as though they are very valuable, which they are. If you don't think they're valuable, neither will anyone else.

Don't forget to use Master Card and Visa to increase your product sales. Charge cards will add 20% to 30% increase in sales. Remind your audience that you offer this service.

It helps to offer a free gift that will be given away at your book table. If you do this they will have to go to the book table to receive their free gift and will most likely consider purchasing something from your selection. One printed page with some helpful hints on your subject matter is enough to get them to respond.

You will find that *packaging your material* will increase your sales. If you have two books and a tape cassette album, put them together and offer them at a price that is *lower* than if they purchased each item *separately.* I put up a small sign at the book table that has a "seminar special." The special is a package offer that contains one of everything sold at the table for a reduced price. This is good for you and it's good for the participant because you will increase your volume sales and the participant will receive a discount.

You can increase your sales by offering books by other authors on the same or related subjects. This is especially helpful in the beginning when you have a limited amount of product to sell. There is a publisher in California who has hundreds of titles for sale at a reasonable cost. They offer a generous discount and their books sell rapidly. If you are interested in increasing your profit margin with a minimum amount of investment, I suggest contacting *Wilshire Books, 120 Sherman Rd., North Hollywood, Ca. 91605*. Ask for their wholesale catalog.

CREATING
A PROFITABLE AFTERMARKET

Selling *additional* books and tapes to your participants
can be a major source of additional income. This can
be done through mail order. Don't miss this opportunity. If you have other items to sell through the mail,
you can *increase your profit margin by 20 or 30 per-
cent*. The determining factor that will convince your
participants of the value of ordering more materials
from you, is to present a high quality speech or seminar. If you give them practical, useful information
and they feel they have received more than their money's worth, you will receive additional sales.

The best way to initiate mail order sales is to *make
sure* you obtain the name and address of every person
who attends your program. Offer a free gift or have
a free drawing for a prize if you have to but get their
names. You can follow-up with a mailing containing
a special offer for additional tapes and books. Don't

miss this opportunity. The back end of your business can be as lucrative as the front end.

If you are going to have an effective aftermarket, you will need to produce additional tapes and books or purchase other authors' materials for resale. A combination of both can be very effective.

You may want to expand your mail order activities to individuals who have not heard you. Millions of people are buying tapes and books through the mail from authors they have never heard of before.

If you are interested in getting into this market, you can learn the nuts and bolts of mail order by purchasing Melvin Power's book HOW TO GET RICH IN MAIL ORDER. It's an excellent book for anyone wishing to get their feet wet in the mail order business. In the beginning I learned more about the mail order business from this book than any other source. I highly recommend it.

A LITTLE KNOWN MARKET
THAT CAN EARN YOU AN EXTRA
$5,000 TO $10,000 PER MONTH

While you are marketing yourself on a local and national level, there is another source of business that can bring in an extra $5,000 to $10,000 per month. This source is the Canadian market.

The speaking and seminar business is in its infancy in Canada. There is a tremendous market there if you are willing to take the time to make contacts. You don't have to do anything different there. You use the same marketing techniques you use in the U.S. If you book one seminar a month in Canada, you can earn an extra $5,000 to $10,000 per month. There is less competition for speakers in Canada so the audience turnout is proportionally higher. It may take you awhile to develop the Canadian market but it will be worth it. Check with booking agents in the major cities of Toronto, Calgary and Vancouver. Send them your demo tape and press kit. Take a vacation there and visit with them personally. If you go on business you can write it off as a business expense.

Canadians are good audiences and wonderful people to work with. They will be receptive to your presentation if you have a high degree of skill and competence in your subject matter. They are no-nonsense people and like you to get to the point and give them full value for their dollar. They *expect* your presentation to be useful, *practical and informative*. They are not as receptive to "motivational" seminars as we are in the U.S. They want you to have *concrete* material that will improve the quality of their life, business or profession.

Some of the best audiences I have worked with have been in Canada. It has always been fun and profitable to work with the Canadians. They are very receptive to purchasing your product if you don't "hustle" them. My product sales in Canada have been above average. You can do well in this market too. Check it out and see for yourself.

A CERTAIN GROUP OF PEOPLE FOUND IN EVERY CITY THAT CAN BE A TREMENDOUS SOURCE OF INCOME

In every city there are dozens of direct sales organizations such as Shaklee, Amway, New-Life, Tupperware, Mary Kay Cosmetics, etc. If marketed properly, they can be a tremendous source of income for the professional speaker.

The advantage of working with these organizations is that they are located in virtually every city in the U.S. If you have another speaking engagement in a certain city, you can book these direct sales organizations back-to-back with your speaking engagement.

It takes a considerable amount of care in marketing these organizations. They tend to be on the defensive when it comes to hiring outside speakers because they have been worked over by so many unscrupulous speakers. It takes time and commitment to book these organizations but, in my opinion, they are well worth the effort. If you treat them with respect, have a quality presentation and a high degree of integrity, you can successfully market these organizations.

The unique advantage of working with these organizations is this: if they like your program and they like you as a person, they will promote you to others within their organization on a *nationwide* basis. The income derived from working with them can be enormous. On the other hand, if you rip them off, they will spread the word faster than a fire in a lumberyard and you'll be out of the market before you can blink your eyes.

Your success in working with these organizations will be in direct proportion to the *trust level* you have built with them. To build this trust level it is essential that you:

1. *Help them before you help yourself*. Let them know *through your actions* that you are more concerned about their needs than yours. They must sense that your primary intention is to help them, not to help yourself. And believe me, they will know right away what your intentions are. Most of them are highly experienced and sophisticated in working with outside speakers. They know all the tricks and they have had a considerable amount of experience in working with the professional as well as the non-professional.

2. *Start on a local basis*. Work with the local organization in your area and build your trust level there. Get to know them personally, find out what their goals are and what problems they are having in achieving these goals. Then find a way to help them solve those

problems through the use of your presentation and materials. Don't try to sell them a packaged or canned program that *you* think they need. Work with them and get to know what *their* needs are.

3. *Do not "hustle" them for product sales*. Most speakers want to work with these organizations so they can sell huge amounts of tapes and books. Don't do it. They are on to this and have built up a resentment towards speakers whose obvious intention is to hustle tapes and books. They *will* purchase your products but only *after* they have been satisfied that you have given them full value for their money and you have not used them as a market for your products. If you give them a quality presentation and satisfy their needs, they will automatically want more of you through your tapes and books. Don't make the mistake of speaking to these organizations with the intention of selling your products. You may get away with it once but they will put you out of the market . . . fast!

What we are saying is simply this: treat them the way you would want to be treated. Don't underestimate them, hustle them, or try to use them to your advantage. Be prepared to be rejected at first but don't let this discourage you. Keep in contact with the local managers or directors and learn about their organization, marketing plan, etc. Make a study of their needs. Find out how you can help them and then offer a specific service. Start out with a free presentation so they can get to know you and build your trust level from there.

Once a bond of friendship has been created and a trust

level established, you will find that most direct sales organizations are the best audiences you can possibly work with. If your program is applicable to their needs, you could develop a working relationship extremely beneficial to all concerned. I encourage you to follow the above suggestions so that you won't miss the opportunity to work with these organizations.

A SIMPLE BUT OVERLOOKED WAY TO EARN $50,000 YOUR FIRST YEAR GIVING FREE SPEECHES!

In this section I am going to show you a step-by-step plan that will enable you to earn over $50,000 your first year giving free speeches. Here's how it works:

I can assume that you have followed the suggestions and instructions presented in the previous sections of this book. You have produced your demo tape and press kit and you have a sufficient assortment of product you can sell at your speeches and seminars.

When starting in the speaking and seminar business, you may encounter some difficulty securing paid speaking assignments. You are probably unknown at this point and understandably there is some resistance on the part of an organization to hire an unknown speaker. This is something that every speaker faces when he or she first starts out to become a professional speaker. As your reputation develops, you will find it easier and easier to secure paid speaking engagements. This is a familiar cycle most individuals go through when they graduate from high school or college. They apply for a job and the employer says "We're looking for someone with experience." The prospective employee says "How can I have experience if you won't hire me?" The same situation applies to the beginning speaker. Most organizations are reluctant to hire speakers who have little experience. But how are you going to have speaking experience if no one will allow you to speak? The answer is to *speak for free*!

Fortunately, there is a way you can speak for free, receive on the job training and on top of that earn over $50,000 per year! It's easier than you think if you will follow the simple instructions I am going to share with you.

First, you will need to contact as many organizations as possible using the procedures and materials outlined in this book. The basic difference here is that you are not asking for a *paid* speaking engagement. In your cover letter you will explain to the potential prospect that you offer an excellent seminar or training program that would be beneficial to their organization. However, you don't want them to take your word for it. You are so sure they will be pleased with your program that you are willing to speak to their organization for *free*. In fact, you will come to them at your expense and put on a *one hour* speech (call it a mini-seminar) to demonstrate your capabilities. In your letter mention that you are so confident they will be satisfied with your presentation that you are sure they will want to book you at a future date for your regular seminar or workshop.

Be sure to sell the *benefits* of your free mini-seminar. Let them know what your presentation will do for *them*. Outline the benefits in a brochure and enclose the brochure with your letter. After your first mini-seminar you can use the brochures from your *previous* seminar to sell the *next* seminar, etc.

Your brochure should be a one page flyer. They are economical to print and easy to read. Let the organization know that you will provide as many brochures as they will need to promote your mini-seminar. The flyer should include a brief biography, your photo, the title of your mini-seminar and most of all, what *benefits* the participants will gain from attending your presentation. You can also include the date, time, place and logistic information.

In return for this all you are asking is that they promote your mini-seminar and turn out an audience of *100 or more people*. Have them encourage their membership to bring guests to your presentation.

This will help to increase the number of participants. You will need 100 or more participants for this to work successfully. If you do a good job with your promotion, they could easily turn out 200 or 300 people.

You may be wondering, "How can I make money speaking for free?" Simple. If you haven't figured it out already, your income will be derived from the sale of your books and tapes. Now don't let the simplicity of this fool you. Keep reading. I'm not finished yet.

Presenting Your Mini-Seminar

Your mini-seminar must be highly *motivational*. Your subject matter should be presented in such a way that the audience *will want more than just a mini-seminar or speech*. To accomplish this, you will have to put together a one hour presentation that contains your *best possible material*. It should include interesting and practical information combined with your best teaching techniques, humorous stories, one liners, anecdotes, etc. Touch on several points that you cover in detail in your regular seminar or workshop. Let them know that the mini-seminar or speech is just the tip of the iceberg. At the same time *give them useful practical information they can leave with and apply immediately*. They came to hear you to receive the *benefits* of your presentation. Make sure they leave with the information you promised them. If you do, they won't forget you.

By the way, while I'm thinking about it, don't try to come up with a new speech every time you speak. Have three or four speeches you know *well* and that have been *polished to perfection*. It is not necessary to come up with something new and original every time you speak. If you keep changing your material, it will sound like you threw something together at the last minute. Work on making your few talks a *theatrical performance*. This is especially true of those you will be giving to sell yourself and your program for future bookings. You can change the title and some of the content to suit your audience but don't try to be original every time. It will work against you. Have fewer speeches but let each one be a masterpiece.

Russell Conwell gave his speech "Acres of Diamonds" over 50,000 times! I know of many speakers who have given the same speech for 25 years or more and are still in demand! One famous speaker told me he has 50 titles and one speech.

Your intention should not be to sell them on your program but to sell them on *you*. It's *you* they really want. If they are moved by *your* presentation and gain benefit from what *you* have to say, they will want more of *you*. It is much easier to sell yourself as a person than it is to sell your program. In fact, I wouldn't mention your program at all except to make occasional reference to the material contained in your program. You want them to know you have additional material to offer but that is not your purpose for being there. *Your purpose is to give them the information they came to get from your mini-seminar or speech.*

Turning Your Mini-Seminar Into Dollars

To turn your mini-seminar into dollars you will have to effectively market your tapes and books. To do this I would suggest bringing *one* book or monograph and *one* tape cassette. Do not bring your tape album or additional books at this time. Save them for your regular seminar. Make a special one hour tape cassette that will be sold exclusively at your mini-seminars or speeches. The title should correspond with the title of your presentation.

After you have finished your mini-seminar, inform your audience that you have brought one tape and one book with you to provide additional information about your subject matter. *Explain how your tape cassette will help them to accomplish certain specifics covered in your presentation*. Give a few examples of what information is on the tape. Then hold up a copy of your book and briefly explain what benefits are contained in the book.

Your entire sales presentation for your product should not last longer than *2 minutes*. You do not want to give them the impression that you are "pitching" them. It must appear that you are just "explaining" what the tape and book are about. There is no need to "pitch" them if you have done a good job with your presentation. They will want more of you and will be willing to spend their money to get it. Remember, *you are a teacher and a speaker*, not a "pitchman."

If you have followed the instructions in the beginning of this section, you will have an audience of at least 100 people. Most of the time it will be more. But let's stick with the minimum figure and see how this works out. If you have presented a dynamic, practical, useful and motivational message, you can expect to sell 30% of your audience a special seminar package.

Your tape cassette should be priced at $10.00. Your book can be priced anywhere between $5.00 and $15.00 for a softcover. Let's use a figure of $7.95.

The price for both items would be $17.95. *Offer them both* for a special price of $16.00. This will give your participants incentive to purchase *both* items.

30% of 100 people is 30 sales. Each sale will average $16.00. This will bring in $480.00. Your cost for materials will be less than $100.00. This would *net* you $380.00. I am not counting individuals that will buy only one tape or book. Average them out and you will still sell about 30% of your audience a complete package.

If you give two presentations a week (some weeks you will do only one, some weeks you will do three or four) you will earn in excess of $39,000 a year. Not bad, but it gets better!

Remember the seminars? The reason you gave your presentation was to sell yourself so they will want to take your regular seminar or workshop. If you present 100 free speeches a year at least 10 of them will result in booking a regular seminar. That's only 10%. It would be impossible to calculate the profits from this because it would depend on your fees, expenses, etc. But conservatively you should *net* a minimum of $2000.00 per seminar. This figure includes tuition charge and product sales.

Ten seminars a year at $2000.00 per seminar would net you an additional $20,000. Add this to the $39,000 you made giving free speeches and *you'll have a net income of over $59,000*! These figures are based on a minimum attendance and realistic product sales.

Imagine what you will earn once you have had a little practice!

Now don't sit there and look for reasons why it won't work. It *will* work because others are doing it year after year. It's going to take a commitment on your part to follow through with your plan but if you are willing to work the plan step-by-step, the profit potential will be well worth it. You'll earn big money and you'll have fun doing it. I know, I've done it!

Have enough confidence in yourself to accept that you can do it. Don't settle for less. Remember, two speeches a week. Make it your number one goal. Do this for one year and you'll be on the road to fame and fortune in the speaking and seminar business. Believe in yourself and others will believe in you. Soon, people will be asking you to speak because you will be well known in the speaking profession. Your income will go from $59,000 to a high 6 figure income. It *can* happen and it *will* happen to you if you get off your metaphysical chair and make your plan and follow through. The only obstacle is procrastination, and you can eliminate that by *starting now*.

SAMPLE SPEAKING AGREEMENT

NAME OF ORGANIZATION_____

NAME OF PERSON TO CONTACT_____TITLE_____

ADDRESS_____CITY_____STATE_____ ZIP_____

BUSINESS PHONE_____HOME PHONE_____

PROGRAM WILL BE HELD AT (ADDRESS)_____

NAME OF NEAREST MAJOR AIRPORT_____

TITLE OF SEMINAR OR SPEECH_____

PRESENTATION DATE(S)_____STARTING TIME(S)_____

LENGTH OF SPEECH OR SEMINAR_____ESTIMATED ATTENDANCE_____

TERMS OF AGREEMENT: Insert financial agreement concerning speaking fee, program tuition, and expenses. Also include information concerning payment to organization if they are to receive a portion of the tuition and/or tape and book sales. Be sure to state that your fees and expenses are due and payable upon completion of the program.

(YOUR NAME) will make his books and tapes available to the program participants. For advance shipment of these materials, the person who will be responsible for receiving them is:

NAME_____ADDRESS_____

CITY_____STATE_____ZIP_____

BUSINESS PHONE_____HOME PHONE_____

DUE TO (YOUR NAME) PUBLISHING AND RECORDING CONTRACT COMMITMENTS, THE ABOVE ORGANIZATION UNDERSTANDS THAT THERE WILL BE NO TAPE RECORDING OR FILMING AT ANY TIME DURING (YOUR NAME) PRESENTATION WITHOUT PRIOR WRITTEN CONSENT.

Minimum period for cancellation of this agreement is 60 (sixty) days prior to the program date. Failure to cancel within this period will impose a cancellation fee of $_____ unless (Your Name) is able to re-book the above date(s).

So that your dates may be guaranteed, a signed copy of this agreement must be returned to the office of (Your Name) within 10 (ten) days.

AUTHORIZED SIGNATURE (Organization)_____DATE_____

(YOUR NAME), by_____DATE_____